W9-BKI-421

# FRANCHISING DREAMS

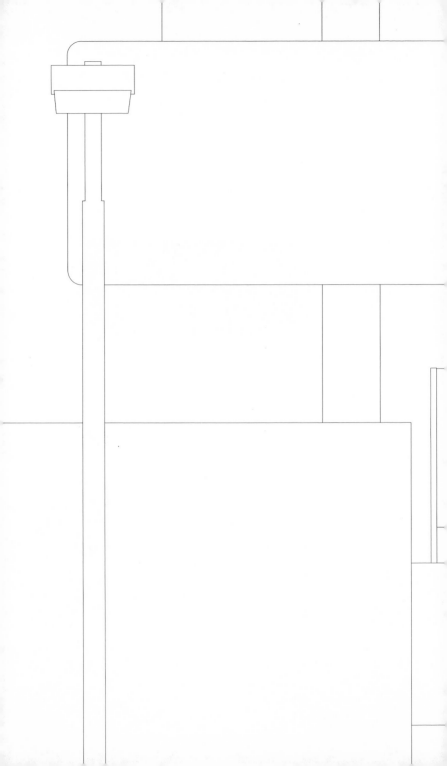

# FRANCHISING DREAMS

THE LURE OF

ENTREPRENEURSHIP

IN AMERICA

## PETER M. BIRKELAND

THE UNIVERSITY OF CHICAGO PRESS
CHICAGO AND LONDON

**PETER M. BIRKELAND** received his Ph.D. in sociology from the University of Chicago. He is the founder of the Birkeland Institute and adjunct professor of strategic management and organization at the Carlson School of Management, University of Minnesota.

The University of Chicago Press, Chicago 60637
The University of Chicago Press, Ltd., London
© 2002 by The University of Chicago
All rights reserved. Published 2002
Printed in the United States of America
10  09  08  07  06  05  04  03  02    1  2  3  4  5
ISBN: 0–226-05190–0 (cloth)

Library of Congress Cataloging-in-Publication Data

Birkeland, Peter M.
    Franchising dreams: the lure of entrepreneurship in America / Peter M. Birkeland.
        p. cm.
    ISBN 0-226-05190-0 (cloth : alk. paper)
    1. Franchises (Retail trade)—United States—Management.
    2. New business enterprises—United States—Management.
    3. Entrepreneurship—United States.   4. Franchises (Retail trade)—United States—Case studies.   I. Title.
    HF5429.235.U5 B57 2002
    658.8'708—dc21                                    2001007061

This book is dedicated to my parents,
Steve and Shelley Birkeland,
and to Gigi.

# CONTENTS

# ACKNOWLEDGMENTS

This book began as a dissertation at the University of Chicago. It is thanks to University of Chicago sociologist Andy Abbott that it did not remain a dissertation. I gave Andy several papers I had written and when we got together to discuss them he said, "Well, in the dissertation you'll want to do it this way, but in the book you'll have to change it and do it a different way." I have tried to follow his advice, the result of which is this book.

Although writing is a solitary experience, the process of creating a book is the result of interactions with many significant people. I received guidance and support from Ed Laumann and Wayne Baker, my teachers, mentors, and friends. Rob Faulkner and Harry Davis both read the manuscript in its formative stages and made many valuable suggestions—Rob, from his keen sociological perspective, and Harry, from his insightful business perspective. Sunday Perry read an early draft of the manuscript and provided perceptive comments about the connection of my work to her industry, financial services. Others who read the manuscript and provided ideas that sharpened it include Jeff Spahn and Kevin Booth. My brother, Steve Birkeland, Jr., and my father and mother, Steve and Shelley Birkeland, not only read the manuscript many times, but also provided encouragement throughout the process.

I received support from Mark Siebert and Dave Hood from the iFranchise Group, and from Stefanie Lenway at the Carlson School, for which I am grateful.

The manuscript was greatly improved by the careful reading and editing of Maia Rigas. Doug Mitchell and his superb colleagues at the University of Chicago Press were enormously helpful.

I could not have written *Franchising Dreams* had it not been for the many franchisees and franchisors who gave their time, shared their insights, and who in many cases opened their lives, experiences, and situations to me. I greatly appreciate their candor, honesty, and goodwill and hope they feel a sense of satisfaction in contributing to this book.

Finally, I have a silent partner who has selflessly given of her talents, providing me with the time needed to complete what has turned out to be a time-consuming process. To Gigi, my wife and friend, thank you.

# CHAPTER 1

## INTRODUCTION

In the Middle Ages, when a sovereign needed to collect tax monies from peasants and other people in the hinterlands, he or she would grant to a high Church official the right to collect the tax. For this right the high Church official would pay the sovereign a lump sum and other special favors—and thus the first franchiselike business arrangement was born.[1] Since the Middle Ages, franchising has been modified and adapted by companies and has grown to become one of the dominant methods to distribute goods and services in the economy. The International Franchise Association, a trade association for franchising, estimates that in the year 2000 in the United States more than 2,000 companies in 75 industries will manage approximately 400,000 franchisees.[2] In turn, these franchisees collectively manage nearly 8 million workers, or approximately 1 out of every 16 employed persons in the U.S. economy. Franchising is so widespread that it is possible to purchase nearly an unlimited array of products and services through franchises, much to the chagrin of its critics, who believe that franchising caused the decline of the family business.[3] The result of this dominance is reflected in the

1. For further discussion on the early history of franchiselike arrangements, see Donald N. Thompson, *Franchise Operations and Antitrust* (Lexington, Mass.: D. C. Heath, 1971).

2. These figures were communicated to me through a source at the International Franchise Association. For industry figures, see also Robert E. Bond, *Bond's Franchise Guide*, 13th ed. (Oakland, Calif.: Source Book Publications, 2001).

3. For an acerbic critic of franchising, see Stan Luxenberg, *Roadside Empires: How the Chains Franchised America* (New York: Viking, 1985).

sheer enormity of retail sales that flow through franchise companies: $1 trillion, or one-third of the entire U.S. gross domestic product.[4]

How did franchising come to play such an important role in the distribution of goods and particularly, of services? What is the experience of franchisors and franchisees and what are the uncertainties they face? How can franchisors control franchisees, and in what ways can franchisees control the franchisor? These are a few of the questions that motivated me to study franchise systems, to work in the day-to-day operations of franchisees in three companies, and to interview franchise insiders over a four-year period.

### THE SCOPE OF FRANCHISING

Although the term "franchising" refers to several different business relationships including distributorships, licensing agreements, leasing plans, and manufacturing and service arrangements,[5] there are primarily two types of franchise systems, product distribution and business-format systems. Product distribution systems were first used by manufacturers of expensive and complex machinery to distribute goods to areas where transportation was costly or access, difficult. In the mid-nineteenth century, Cyrus McCormick's harvester machine and I. M. Singer's sewing machine were both distributed through a franchise-like relationship. This particular distribution method, in which the manufacturer utilizes the franchise outlet as a conduit to the final consumer, is still widely used today by automobile manufacturers and their dealers. Generally, manufacturers allow franchisees a wide berth to operate the unit as they see fit, affording the franchisee autonomy in operations, management, marketing, and advertising. This is why the consumer experience in terms of hours of operation, prices, layout of the building, tactics of sales managers, and other services may vary

---

4. Personal communication with International Franchise Association Director of Public Relations Terry Hill, 14 September 1999.

5. Louis W. Stern and Adel El-Ansary, *Marketing Channels*, 4th ed. (Englewood Cliffs, N.J.: Prentice Hall, 1992), 342–56.

significantly from one dealer to another—even among car dealers of the same make.

However, for many people the term "franchising" is synonymous with McDonald's, Burger King, Jiffy Lube, and other retailers in the service economy. These well-known franchisors are business-format franchisors, a type of franchise system in which a franchisee operates a unit under the company's trademark and delivers a proscribed set of services under the company's guidelines and "suggested" prices. Business-format franchising emerged during the 1930s when oil refiners such as Sun Oil found that mass distribution of its gasoline was not profitable because it was a generic product. To avoid a price war, Sun Oil developed name-brand recognition for its outlets, and bundled (and sold) support services to franchisees.[6] In business-format franchising, companies train franchisees in operations and provide on-going advice, marketing, advertising, and other support services to them. Franchisees in turn pay an up-front fee for the right to operate the unit under the company's trademark, and they finance the construction or purchase of their franchise unit and pay for all capital upgrades and improvements. In addition, franchisees pay continuing royalties based upon gross sales.

Because business-format franchisors sell a business concept—a trademark that implies consistency of standards, operating methods, products, and services—the franchise unit itself is a profit center. In fact, it is both a distribution channel used to facilitate the movement of goods and services and a profit center. The dual nature of business-format franchising and the adaptability of companies to market manifold services and products using franchising has fueled the growth of the strategy. Most academic work on this subject has focused on business-format franchising and especially on the issue of why a company would pursue franchising as a way to distribute goods and services, rather than own and manage all retail outlets.

6. A well-researched history of franchise growth in the United States is provided by Thomas Dicke in *Franchising in America: The Development of a Business Method, 1840–1980* (Chapel Hill: University of North Carolina Press, 1992).

Franchising was initially considered a temporary strategy deployed by small companies in response to inefficient capital markets. The capital-acquisition explanation argued that companies only pursue franchising because it allows them to expand quickly without taking on debt or relinquishing control through stock offerings.[7] Over time, companies would become wholly-owned chains and capture the full revenue stream. But the temporary nature of franchising has not been borne out and a second explanation, principal-agent theory, claims that franchising persists because it solves or greatly reduces problems of shirking inherent in vertical delegation.[8] That is, franchising generally occurs in situations where the franchisee is geographically distant from the franchisor and therefore monitoring performance and behavior is difficult or costly. Since franchisors cannot directly oversee franchisee operations, "it pays to devise control mechanisms which give the franchisee an incentive to be efficient—to avoid shirking and excessive consumption of leisure."[9] One such control mechanism is a royalty payment, which not only gives the franchisee the right to operate under the firm's trademark and receive managerial advice but also motivates the franchisor to monitor and police the quality of all franchisees. Both parties have an economic incentive to control those aspects of the relationship that have the greatest impact on their incomes: Franchisees control the day-to-day operation of their enterprise while the franchisor controls the trademark value. Franchising, then, is an efficient solution to the organizational problem of control since there

7. For the first discussion of franchising from this perspective, see A. R. Oxenfeldt and A. O. Kelly, "Will Successful Franchise Systems Ultimately Become Wholly Owned Chains?" *Journal of Retailing* 44 (1969): 69–87.

8. For a very good introduction to principal-agent theory and its wide applicability to numerous problems, see John W. Pratt and Richard J. Zeckhauser, eds., *Principals and Agents: The Structure of Business* (Boston, Mass: Harvard Business School Press, 1985). For the classic statement of principal-agent theory applied to franchising, see Paul H. Rubin, "The Theory of the Firm and the Structure of the Franchise Contract," *Journal of Law and Economics* 21 (1978): 223–33.

9. Rubin, "Theory of the Firm," 226.

are economic incentives in place to bind both parties to the trademark.

But notice that, from the principal-agent perspective, organizational control only pertains to franchisors controlling franchisees, not to franchisees controlling the franchisor. It is an ideological assumption that "shirking and excessive leisure" will be undertaken by franchisees and not franchisors—an assumption that can be put to an empirical test. Moreover, it is not clear that economic incentives are sufficient to ensure that franchise systems are controlled; indeed, one could easily imagine that recruiting the right people to become franchisees may make the system easier to control.

## METHODOLOGY

I began my research on issues of control within franchise systems and on conflicts and conflict resolution in situations in which the people involved are geographically dispersed. I wanted to determine if the economic incentives put forth by principal-agent theory were more effective than social mechanisms, such as selective recruitment. To discover the answers to these questions, I employed a theoretically grounded approach and participated in the frontline operations of franchisees in three companies, referred to here by the pseudonyms of King Cleaners, Sign Masters, and Star Muffler. I also conducted structured interviews and network analysis with franchisees and with the CEO and other senior executives of each company. In addition to specific research on franchise participants at the three companies, I attended seminars by franchise consultants on how to make a business "franchiseable," as well as franchise expositions at which hundreds of companies provide business opportunities and recruit new franchisees. I also interviewed other franchise executives, lawyers, and franchise experts. The information I gathered has rounded out my knowledge of the world of the franchising strategy and its pitfalls.

Although I carried out the research over a four-year period, one of the critical findings occurred during the very early stages when I first began my ethnography. I had worked for several weeks in the operations of a franchisee with whom I was acquainted at King Cleaners when he invited me to attend a regional conference sponsored by the company. King Cleaners provides commercial and residential cleaning and maintenance services, and this would be an opportunity for me to meet other franchisees, corporate managers, suppliers, and others involved in the industry. At the end of the first day, a hot July afternoon, a crowd of maybe one hundred franchisees stood impatiently in the convention center parking lot waiting for King Cleaners to unveil a window-washing unit. A few minutes earlier the crowd had been jovial and boisterous, but now an uneasy silence quieted even the most outspoken and skeptical franchisees.

Tom from "Central"—the corporate offices of King Cleaners—managed with just one direct question to unearth a profile of franchisees and capture the critical problem the company faced in managing them: how to motivate franchisees to follow the company's guidelines. For the past twenty minutes, Tom had been enthusiastically describing the features and benefits of a new window-washing unit the company developed. The washer unit was housed on a trailer that could easily be transported behind a van or other vehicle, and it displayed the signature colors and logo of King Cleaners. Although the trailer was streamlined in shape, it was still rather large—about the size and shape of a horse trailer. King Cleaners believed that the new window-washer would not only solve several technical problems franchisees faced but would also be more efficient and less labor-intensive than washing windows by hand, the current method used by franchisees.

The demonstration aimed to persuade franchisees to purchase the window-washer, and Tom explained that it was simple to operate and cost-effective to own. The franchisees, however, were decidedly less enthusiastic than Tom, despite the presence of a gleaming new piece of machinery.

In the face of rising antagonism, Tom explained how the unit operated. "The window-washer utilizes tap water from, say, the garden faucet," he explained loudly, "and then it runs through a series of filters that filter out all traces of iron. You see, it's the iron that causes windows to streak and spot, so by removing the iron we can spray directly onto the windows. You don't have to send an employee around to squeegee each window by hand. With this unit they can just spray off the dirt and move on."

"How big is the tank?" a franchisee yelled from the back of the crowd.

"It'll hold a hundred gallons," Tom replied.

"Well, how long will it take to fill a one-hundred-gallon tank?" he asked.

"About thirty minutes or so," Tom answered.

"Yeah, well, in thirty minutes I can have all the windows cleaned by hand," the franchisee said with a look of triumph.

Bolstered by the complaints of the one outspoken franchisee, the quiet grumbling of franchisees around me grew more vocal in their antagonism of Tom.

"Man! Can you imagine driving that thing around some of these suburbs? You couldn't do it without taking out a couple of parked cars," one franchisee joked.

"Yeah, and where the heck do you park it? You can't leave that in your driveway," said another franchisee.

"What's worse," broke in a third franchisee, "is that if you leave it at a warehouse, someone can just hook it up and drive off with it."

"I don't know," said the first franchisee, "it seems like a helluva lot of trouble for the window market. What are they asking for it, did they say?"

"No, he hasn't said yet," replied an onlooker.

"It must be expensive then," replied the first franchisee. "Hey," he turned toward Tom, "how long is the hose?"

"You mean the garden hose?" asked Tom.

"No, the power hose from the washer," he replied.

"Oh," said Tom, "it's one hundred feet."

"That ain't gonna be long enough. You can hardly get from the street to anywhere with a hundred feet of hose."

"We realize that one hundred feet is inadequate, and we're working on it," Tom said. "This is just a prototype of the unit, and we still have some changes to make. I think once you see how easy it is to operate you'll be satisfied, so let me start with one of the windows over here."

Tom started the washer unit and washed a large eight-by-twelve-foot window in about thirty seconds merely by spraying it from top to bottom.

"Now," Tom explained, "We'll let this dry, and you'll be amazed—there won't be any streaks or spots. But you can see how easy it is to operate. There's no need to haul a ladder from one window to the next because you can do everything from the ground. Not only is it more efficient for you, but it's safer for your employees." Tom turned to the crowd. "Who wants to give this a try next?"

There was an awkward moment of silence as the franchisees stood hesitant, meek, and timid. They shifted their eyes toward the ground, shuffled their feet, and avoided direct eye contact with Tom.

Again, in a louder voice, Tom called out, "Come on, doesn't anyone want to try it?"

Finally, after a long pause one franchisee stepped forward and volunteered to try the new unit. There was a collective sigh of relief among the crowd of onlookers. But he was the only volunteer of the day, and Tom ended the demonstration shortly thereafter.

"Well," said Tom, "I'll leave some information here, and if you have any questions I'd be happy to answer them."

### EARLY INSIGHTS

It is often the case in the first stages of ethnographic research that the initial insights about a phenomenon prove, in the long run, to be accurate. The profile of franchisees that I discovered at King Cleaners during the window-washing demonstration surprised me because I had thought that franchisees would be aggressive, self-motivated, and entrepreneurial. Instead, what I saw at the demonstration cast doubt on my assumptions about that profile. Franchisees appeared to be

- business owners rather than entrepreneurs;
- risk-averse rather than risk takers;
- outspoken and critical of new initiatives rather than support-ive of new programs and services; and
- averse to capital investments and upgrades rather than eager to make them.

The franchisee reactions at the demo also highlighted the seri-ous issues facing companies that franchise concerning how to best manage and motivate franchisees.

I decided to expand my research from the one franchisee with whom I was acquainted, Larry, to the other franchisees at King Cleaners. Toward that end I contacted the CEO, Bill Parker, with a research proposal to study conflicts in arm's length contracts. He immediately rejected the proposal on the grounds that the "timing" was not right, that the company lacked sufficient funds to undertake a research project, and that managers had already spent a significant amount of time working with researchers from another university. He did offer to provide any public com-pany documents that might be helpful and, as an added benefit, invited me to lunch with another senior executive and himself some six months later.

Since the lunch was so far off, I continued to work with Larry, the King Cleaners franchisee. My circle of acquaintances widened as he introduced me to the area franchise manager and other franchisees in the system. In each introduction, he indicated, with a certain amount of pride, that I was a gradu-ate student at the University of Chicago and also that I had an upcoming meeting with Parker. Taken together, these two state-ments increased my credibility, but it was the future meeting with Parker in particular that added the requisite legitimacy and importance to open many doors at King Cleaners.

As the CEO of a company with revenues in the billions and thousands of franchisees, Parker had tremendous demands upon his time. The fact that he chose to spend even one hour with me signaled to others in the company that my project had merit and that they should therefore cooperate with me. By the time I met with Parker, I had months of fieldwork experience with several franchisees, I had attended the regional franchise association meeting (at which the window-washer unit was demonstrated), and I had gained some understanding of the fundamental uncertainties of the franchise strategy.

Going into my lunch with Parker, I was confident that my research project would not be merely academic and theoretical in content but could be valuable for the company and franchisees. I called the senior executive who would be joining us for lunch about a week prior to the meeting to ask for advice on how to gain Parker's support for the project. To my surprise, he responded, "Don't even bring up franchising. Parker believes that our business is headed in a different direction and, quite frankly, he's not interested in the franchise side of the business." My plan to gain access to executives, managers, and franchisees suddenly appeared in jeopardy.

In retrospect, nearly all that I learned about franchising I had known by the time I met Parker and the senior executive for lunch, but it took me many years to realize that. We had lunch at the corporate offices of King Cleaners, and during our several hours together the conversation covered many topics. But despite his apparent interest in intellectual matters and his sincerity, the CEO was wholly unreceptive to my studying the company, especially from a sociological perspective. Finally, in desperation, I asked him point-blank for the one thing I wanted.

"I want to study the franchise side of the business," I stated.

"The franchise side?" he asked. "Why?"

"I'm interested in how conflicts are resolved and how the system is controlled," I replied. As an afterthought, I said, "I don't think my project will take any managerial time from the corporation. I've already spent time working alongside franchisees and that's what I'd like to continue doing."

"I see," he said as he removed his glasses and leaned back in his chair. "I can't prevent you from talking to franchisees. They're free to speak with you if they want."

"Oh, I didn't realize that. I won't if you think it's a bad idea."

"No, if that's what you want to do then you're free to do that. You see, a manager will do what you want, but he won't work very hard. A franchisee will work hard, but he won't do what you want."

Parker left me with that valuable thought, which highlighted exactly what I needed to understand. In the end, my access to King Cleaners's franchisees was never in jeopardy because Parker could not prevent me from talking to them nor could he prevent franchisees from speaking with me. Franchisees are independent contractors, and they are free to speak with whomever they choose. More important, my access was assured by the very tension and underlying conflict that I sought to understand. Franchisees were more than willing to speak with me because they wanted "their" side of the story to be known. Any strategy by Parker to limit my access, say, by warning franchisees in a memo, would certainly backfire for this very reason. Parker knew all too well that the boundaries of the franchise side of the business were permeable and that King Cleaners lacked the ability to control many aspects of a franchisee's business, including blocking out infiltrators like me from the environment.

Gaining access to Sign Masters was not nearly as involved as that of King Cleaners, in part because the company was an order of magnitude smaller. Sign Masters was a start-up in the relatively new computer-generated sign industry, and when I began my research the company had revenues of $1 million and thirty-four franchisees. It went downhill precipitously from that point forward, and by the time I completed my project the company was nearly insolvent. I met the CEO, Stu Beyer, at a trade show and during the course of our conversation he became interested in my project.

In hindsight, I understand now that Beyer was desperate and grasping for anything that would help him be more competitive. But his interest was genuine, and he wanted me to speak with franchisees, to interact with them, and to learn the business—in complete contrast to the response of Parker, who had merely acquiesced. Soon after our initial conversation, I followed up with a letter and proposal, and I was granted full access by Beyer to himself, to his executive team, and to the franchisees.

Finally, another franchisor steered me toward Mark Spinelli, CEO of Star Muffler. Star Muffler was a player in the muffler and brake industry. In this highly competitive market, Star Muffler was in the middle of the pack, with thirty-seven franchisees and revenues of $20 million annually. I approached Spinelli with a letter of introduction and an outline of my research proposal, but since I was introduced by an executive known to him my project was given serious consideration immediately. I clarified my project during a phone conversation and met with him at the corporate offices to work through the details. Spinelli was extremely generous with his time, candid about the business and the issues he faced, and provided full access to his executive team and franchisees.

The way that an ethnographer gains entrance to an organization is often telling, and the exit can be equally revealing. Eventually, all ethnographic researchers wear out their welcome. They do so not so much because of a personality flaw or because they are viewed as a threat, but rather because the constraints that academics and business people face are so different. A business person's time horizon is often measured in hours, and in order for them to justify the time the research project takes—time they could spend on more pressing and important tasks—they need ideas, solutions, and results that immediately help them with the day-to-day demands of the business.

Academic research by nature (and design) is far more cautious, and the results of any inquiry can follow the initial data collection—interviews, surveys, and so on—by months or years. Although I believed this book would be instructive to many people in the franchise systems I studied, my insights crystallized only over the course of my research. At the time when I was participating in the franchise operations, my ideas were in the formative stages and were not helpful to the participants. The waning importance of my work became apparent during a discussion with John, my sponsor at King Cleaners. Walking through a parking lot on a cold January evening, John was uncharacteristically silent. Finally, when we reached our parting point he turned to me and said,

"Peter, what are you going to do with all this information?"

"What information?"

"All the data you've been collecting. What are you going to do with it?"

I sensed that he was afraid I would make the information public so I responded, "Oh, I don't have that much information."

"Well, you've been writing notes since last May! You must have a book by now."

"No," I laughed, "maybe a pamphlet. I plan on writing up the results for my dissertation. I don't think that many people will read it. And, of course, I'll share everything with you."

"Well," he said, "if you really want to know about franchising, you should buy a franchise."

And that was the last conversation I had with John. Once it became clear that I was no longer instrumental to his goal of selling more franchises he became less receptive to my research project. Buying a franchise was the farthest thing from my mind since my goal was to learn about franchising as an observer of several different systems, not as a participant in one particular system. Through my theoretically grounded approach I learned about the uncertainties plaguing companies that franchise, and even though King Cleaners, Sign Masters, and Star Muffler differ in size, revenues, number of franchisees, products, technologies, and profit margins, they share many characteristics in common. These characteristics include

- low barriers to entry,
- numerous competitors,
- low switching costs for consumers,
- episodic rather than recurrent transactions,
- limited name-brand recognition,
- reliance on part-time and hourly employees, and
- limited alternative suppliers.

Although these characteristics are endemic to all companies that operate in turbulent environments, franchise companies have the additional problems of having to sell franchise units and provide services to franchisees. Clearly, it is a challenging environment and one that I explore more fully in the following chapters.

OVERVIEW

In chapter 2, "Franchise Fundamentals," I explore three basic components that are features of all franchise systems: royalties, trademarks, and long-term contracts. I show how these components function and, in particular, how they impact franchisee survival rates. In chapters 3, 4, and 5, I provide detailed accounts of the nature of work franchisees carry out at King Cleaners, Sign Masters, and Star Muffler, respectively. In these chapters I share my firsthand account of working in the day-to-day operations of franchisees, and I document the sources of uncertainty they face. In chapter 6, I introduce a typology of franchisees that cuts across all three companies. The three types of franchisee, which I term "neo-franchisees," "disillusioned franchisees," and "sideliners," present managerial problems for franchisors and have consequences for other franchisees in each company. In chapter 7, I address the causes for differential franchisee success and, in particular, the critical role that social capital plays in franchisee performance. In chapter 8, I explore more fully franchising from the franchisor's perspective. What are some of the uncertainties they face in recruiting, monitoring, and managing franchisees? I return in chapter 9 to the original problem of how to control people who are geographically distant from corporate headquarters and thus cannot be supervised on-site. Are economic incentives enough to bind parties together, or does the success of franchising hinge upon social mechanisms, social interactions, and trust?

What follows then is an account of my experiences working with franchisees in three franchise systems. I cannot claim that my cases represent franchising in its entirety, nor would I claim anything like a scientific approach or a random sample in choosing cases to carry out my research. Even so, an ethnographic approach was never meant to substitute for statistical analysis, and the strength of my approach lies not in precise estimates of some particular phenomenon but rather in a richly detailed description of people, the situations they encounter, and environments in which they find themselves. Toward that end, I hope this book will provide a sociological understanding of franchising both to those familiar with the strategy as franchisees or franchisors as well as to those who are familiar with it only as consumers.

# CHAPTER 2

FRANCHISE FUNDAMENTALS

Franchising is utilized by a wide variety of companies in numerous industries to sell goods and services through retail outlets. One may naturally ask, are there any features that franchise companies have in common, any characteristics that set franchising apart from other strategies? It appears that there are, for a franchise executive remarked at a Congressional hearing some thirty years ago, "I would say that we have more in common with other franchising firms, regardless of their industry, than we do with nonfranchising firms in our own industry. Our problems of motivation, training, business development, of franchisee-franchisor relations are not shared by firms that simply sell their products to a totally independent operator or deal with employees in company-owned outlets."[1]

On the surface, this statement arouses incredulity, since franchising is the chosen strategy for a wide variety of companies that conduct business across many industries. How could such widely varying companies have so much in common? Are the same issues of motivation, training, and business development still present today? I asked an executive at Star Muffler whether the company had more in common with other companies that franchise or with companies that don't franchise.

"Well, I think that first, we have the most in common with other companies in our industry that franchise because we're

1. Donald N. Thompson, *Franchise Operations and Antitrust* (Lexington, Mass.: D. C. Heath, 1971), 5.

competing for the same person to become a franchisee," he explained. "Then we have more in common with other companies that franchise, regardless of industry. Lastly, we have something in common with the companies in our industry, and other companies not in our industry—well, we face the same general problems that all companies face."

Today, franchisors generally agree that the franchising strategy unifies them within a common worldview. The issues, problems, and risks inherent in the strategy are common to those who pursue it. The elements faced by franchise companies include both constraints and opportunities and derive from a set of features that are the core of franchising. At a minimum, these fundamentals involve the trademark, royalties, and long-term contracts. I analyzed how these elements function at King Cleaners, Sign Masters, and Star Muffler.

## TRADEMARK VALUE? WHAT VALUE?

Doug and George were more than partners in their King Cleaners franchise. Brothers-in-law, they had known each other for more than thirty years, and they had shared similar corporate backgrounds. Both were in their early fifties, and their move into franchising marked the start of a new and challenging career for them.

"Why did you buy this franchise?" I asked.

"It sure wasn't for the money," replied George.

"Yeah," quipped Doug, "George was the national sales manager at a Fortune 500 company before we did this, and he made a nice six-figure salary. Right, George?"

"Yep."

"You know," said Doug, "our employees think we're made of money. No, really, they just think we have wads of cash in our pockets, but they don't even understand that we're this close to failing." Doug held his thumb and forefinger close together. "They think that we live in a big house and drive a Mercedes or something."

"But," interrupted George, "to answer your question, I was tired of traveling all the time and being away from my family.

Doug here had the idea to buy a franchise, and he convinced me to join him. We knew we didn't want to be in retail; we wanted a business-to-business franchise and that's what this is. So I quit my six-figure job for this. Now I can count the figures on one hand—and that's with a decimal place!" he laughed.

"For me," stated Doug, "it was a midlife crisis. I was doing a lot of technical work, mainly with computers at a large corporation in Chicago, and I just thought that was it for me. I couldn't see myself doing that for another twenty years."

"Well," I asked, "how has it been?"

"It sure got off to a rocky start," replied Doug. "I remember thinking right after we bought this thing, 'Boy! Did we ever make a mistake! This is the biggest mistake of our lives!' And, of course, our wives are sisters, so, I mean, if we go down, both families go down. There's no escape. We have to go through with it. What else are we going to do?"

"What led you to think it was a big mistake?"

"Well, George can tell you," continued Doug. "Remember your first day selling contracts?"

"Oh, yeah," agreed George. "See, we figured we had a pretty good business plan. With my sales experience, I would be the sales guy, and Doug here would take care of the administrative and technical end of the business. So, anyway, the first week we bought the franchise, I go out making sales calls on some of these corporate clients. I'm driving around in my car, and I see a nice account, perfect for us, so I go in and make an appointment with the contract manager. Well, I'm in his office making a sales pitch, and suddenly the guy snaps out of a trance and goes, 'King Cleaners! You guys are already cleaning the place!' I was shocked because I knew *we* weren't cleaning the place. So I tried to cover my tracks and said something like, 'Gee, ah, I guess you're right.' So I hustle right out of there and get on the phone to the franchisor and say, 'Hey John, I just got out of a place in my territory, and one of our own guys is already cleaning it!' and he says to me, 'Well, you know, that could be. There are no exclusive territories.' 'WHAT?!' I ask him. I was stunned by what he said. 'What are you talking about?' And he says the same thing, there aren't any exclusive territories. And I'm thinking to myself, this has got to be a joke because I bought an exclusive territory."

"So, right away I call up my attorney, and he looks at the contract document I had signed, and he tells me that there aren't any exclusive territories. I'm looking at my contract as I speak to the guy and I say to him, 'Are you looking at my contract? Do you have the map?' And he says, 'Yeah, your territory is not exclusive.' I have a map of the whole metropolitan area, and my area is highlighted in pink marker. And my attorney says, 'Your contract says the county and state, including, but not limited to your area.' OK, but everything King Cleaners said to me in the sales pitch implied that I had an exclusive territory. I never asked them point-blank if I had an exclusive territory, but they never told me that I didn't, and they even led me to believe that I did have one, what with the map and my area outlined in pink! In fact, had I known that the territory was not exclusive, I would have thought twice about buying the franchise. I would not have bought it."

"That's funny," I responded, "I always thought there was a noncompete clause."

"So did we!" exclaimed Doug. "We're doing OK now, but at the time we were pretty upset about it. It still bothers me. Basically, they lied to us."

"Are there very many other franchisees in your area?"

"There's a ton," declared Doug. "Most of them are pretty poor quality and are not really competitors, but there are guys that come in from other territories, and some of them are formidable competitors. If you look at our area, we're right in the middle of the largest office complexes in Chicago outside of the Loop. There are a lot of incentives for guys to come in here and steal our clients."

"Do you go into other territories?"

"I won't go into another franchisee's area if I think they're good," said George. "But if they show poor quality or if they choose to compete in my area, then I have no problem with competing in their territory."

"What about John, the distributor who oversees the franchisees in this area?" I asked.

"What about John?" returned Doug.

"What does he say about franchisees going into each other's area?"

"He doesn't say anything. He lets franchisees work it out. If they can't work it out, he'll propose a solution, but he could care less where franchisees get their clients," Doug said.

Intrafirm competition is an unanticipated consequence of operating under the same trademark. This result is somewhat surprising because trademarks have been called the "cornerstone" of franchising,[2] and rightly so. They are a form of intellectual property as well as the primary symbols that differentiate companies within the same industry. Of course, they also connote a standard of quality and consistency of product or service. If the trademark value is high, franchisees enjoy name-brand recognition and perhaps higher sales, loyal customers, and a more qualified labor supply. Franchisors, too, reap the benefits of increased sales and might also be able to sell more franchise units to higher qualified franchisees. A high trademark value thus allows both franchisees and franchisors to accrue higher than average profits, while a devalued trademark hurts both parties. Because their economic fates remain so closely tied to the trademark, it is believed that both parties will work to keep the value high. But competition among franchisees changes the value of the trademark somewhat.

"Is the trademark valuable?" I asked.

"It is for King Cleaners," replied Doug. "I mean, we thought it was valuable before we got into this thing, that's why we bought the franchise. But most of the value is because of us, because we've made it valuable."

"I don't know about that," countered George. "I think the trademark has some value, even at the beginning. I'd sure hate to have to figure out a way to get in to see some of these contract

2. William J. Keating, *Franchising Adviser* (Colorado Springs: Shepard's/McGraw-Hill, 1987), 151.

managers on my own. King Cleaners is at least a name they recognize. So I think there is some value in the trademark."

"Yeah," Doug replied, "it has some value, but it had a lot less value than I thought it would have."

"Yeah, I agree with that," said George.

So did many other franchisees. Trademark value is such as integral part of franchising that I discussed it with every franchisee and franchisor with whom I came into contact. Although I expected franchisees to value their own trademark highly, most of them expressed opinions similar to those of Doug and George.

"I thought I would start ahead of the competition," complained a Sign Masters franchisee, "but realistically, there was no value, or even negative value. Now there is value, but it's because of things I did."

A franchisee from Star Muffler added, "It does not bring in much business, and whatever business it does bring in, I suppose it helps people feel more secure. But right now I feel that it is my business—that it's my name on the front because the numbers would be the same. About 80 percent of the business is repeat over the last year, and I probably only get one or two new customers a week because of the name."

While it might seem that intrafirm competition would mostly apply to King Cleaners because franchisees seek out customers, at Sign Masters and Star Muffler there is competition because customers seek out franchisees.

"Customers come in here all the time and complain about the prices," said a Star Muffler franchisee. "They'll say, 'Why are your prices so much higher than the other Star Muffler guy?' So you have to match the other guy's price."

But the cost of labor and capital equipment to franchisees can differ markedly because of varying economic conditions at the time when franchisees entered the market, differences in location, and different strategies franchisees pursue. Although franchisees are free to sell their services at any price they desire, in practice they have to sell at prices similar to those of other franchisees in the system. And these prices are normally influenced by the franchisor through the use of the term "suggested price" in advertising and marketing materials. Needless to say, the prices for services offered by Star Muffler is a major source of contention among franchisees.

FORUM FOR FRANCHISEES

The importance of pricing is never far from any franchisee's thoughts, and the issue was likely to emerge any time franchisees gathered together. One such gathering promoted by the franchisor is a franchisee advisory board meeting, a monthly event where franchisors meet select franchisees to discuss marketing and advertising issues, to help franchisors gauge franchisee attitudes, and to get feedback on programs before they are instituted systemwide. I attended several advisory board meetings at Star Muffler, but no matter what agenda CEO Mark Spinelli set, the discussion would invariably return to the issue of prices.

"I don't know about our pricing structure," complained a Star Muffler franchisee at a franchisee advisory meeting. "It seems that we're trying to be a discount shop. I mean, we lower our prices, and Midas and everyone else follows so there isn't any advantage. We should *raise* our prices, and then maybe everyone else will follow."

"Nah," answered another franchisee, "Midas tried that a couple of years ago. They raised their prices from $79.95 to $99.95 for brake pads, but no one followed, so they came back down."

"The problem is not the price," CEO Mark Spinelli remarked, "but in the way franchisees handle customers. When somebody calls, you don't quote a price over the phone. That's the wrong approach, that's not the Star Muffler approach. In our system, you quote the job, all the things included like the warranty and inspection, and the discount—not the total price."

"Yeah, but Mark, you know, the guy is just shopping price."

"Look," Spinelli rejoined, "everybody assumes that the customer is rational and researched, but he isn't. We see these people an hour later in the shop."

The conversation changed from pricing policy to figuring out what other franchisees in the room actually charged.

"Say, Rocky, what are you charging for a brake job?" asked one franchisee. Rocky was one of the most influential franchisees in the system, in part because he owned several Star Muffler shops, but mostly because of his irreverent, antimanagerial attitude.

"$99.99," replied Rocky.

"$99.99! Shit, that's above list. No wonder your profit margins are so high."

"Fuck the customer."

"What about an oil change?"

"$9.99."

"You're joking."

"No, I'm not," Rocky declared. "$9.99."

"Why? That doesn't even cover the cost of the oil and filter."

"Hey, I can do what I want."

Rocky is right. He can do what he wants—within limits—but his actions impact everyone else in the system because franchisees are interdependent. They are interdependent precisely because of the trademark. Certainly, the trademark can provide benefits to franchisees, but it also constrains them in both obvious and not-so-obvious ways. For instance, since franchisors strive for consistency within their system, they demand that all franchise units look the same, that each unit use the same colors and logo, and that each unit have nearly the same physical layout. Often, franchise units are located in geographical areas with similar characteristics, say, at the edge of a strip mall or at the intersection of two major highways. So franchise units not only look identical, but also are similarly situated in the environment. Franchisors also expect franchisees to deliver their services in a proscribed fashion. Franchisees are trained to operate in the same way: they apply the same technology, use the same stream of inputs, and deliver the same advertising message to customers.

Even something as straightforward as standard operating hours may have unintended consequences. For example, one franchisee mentioned how a franchisor's push for standards negatively impacted nearly all African American franchisees.

"Franchisors have to let franchisees adapt to their market," he stated, "they can't just dictate the same things to everybody. When I was a franchisee in the restaurant business the chain had hours of operation from something like 11 A.M. until 11 P.M. Well, things don't really get hopping in the black community until after 11 P.M. and that was reflected in our sales. They made us feel like we were bad at business. They would publish the sales amounts for all franchisees—just like they do here—and the blacks always had the lowest numbers. I mean, there it was in black and white, month after month, and we were always lagging behind. We finally convinced them that our markets were different—an urban black market is not the same as a suburban white market. And once we did that and were allowed to stay open 'til 2 A.M., our numbers improved. But getting them to change was not easy."

Consistency may benefit the chain, but it can hurt individual franchisees, as the example above illustrates. In nearly all respects, the standardization that franchisors strive for—the hallmark of franchising—ensures that franchisees will be perfect substitutes for each other. No wonder franchisors believe the trademark to be valuable. Stu Beyer of Sign Masters explained, "The trademark is more valuable than most people are willing to apply to it. We have a great name, and there are a lot of benefits that come with the name, like the license and buying power. People want to assign market share to the name, but you can't do that. I'll tell you one thing, though, the name has more value in the market than the individual would have on their own, that's for sure."

Despite the fact that trademarks standardize franchise units, increase franchisee interdependencies, lead to competition with others in the system, and make franchise units into perfect substitutes, there are solutions to these constraints. One strategy that successful franchisees adopt is to minimize price or service considerations and focus instead on relationships. "The only reason my clients stay with me is because they like me," a franchisee from King Cleaners said. "They like my personality, like to do business with me. I'm not the cheapest guy around, but my clients like me."

Franchisors recognized the importance of building relationships. As Mark Spinelli said, "Franchisees will tell you that consumers are price-sensitive, but it's not true. People don't shop price. They look for value, and they look for someone to trust. If your shop is clean, you greet a person as they come through the door, treat them with respect and fairness, and explain to them the options for their car, they'll buy your service. No one is going to leave the shop to drive down the road and look for a better bargain if they're treated fairly."

But for those franchisees that are unable to capitalize on relationships and cannot escape competition with perfect substitutes, the trademark is as much a shackle as it is a key to profits.

## ROYALTIES: THE LIFEBLOOD OF FRANCHISING

During a seminar for entrepreneurs contemplating franchising, a consultant highlighted the importance of royalties. "We suggest that you collect royalties weekly," he stated, "only because it is inconvenient to collect them hourly." The budding franchisors laughed at his joke, yet it underscored the importance of royalties within franchise systems. Royalties are the key to successful franchising because they provide a steady stream of income to the franchisor. A senior executive at King Cleaners described how even a small payment was critical: "We really drill it into the franchisee's head to pay the royalty on the tenth of every month. We tell them, 'even if you only do fifty dollars in one month, you still have to pay the royalty,' because we want that money."

"What is that money used for?" I asked.

"What is it used for?" he repeated. "It's ours to use any way we want! We use it to keep our operations going, and we funnel it back into the franchise system. That's a crazy question."

"OK, let me say it a different way. There are some academics who think that the royalty payment is a payment to make sure the franchisor polices the quality of the other franchisees. What do you think about this idea?"

"I think that's a crazy idea. It's ours to use to develop the system." The responses from the other franchisors were essentially the same. Stu Beyer from Sign Masters, when asked the same question about a franchisor's responsibility to monitor the system, exclaimed in a rare outburst, "No, not at all! It's compensation back to the licensor to hold him away from the market— to keep company-owned units and other franchisees out. Our royalty income is used to pay overhead and salaries, and it also provides training and support." A second franchisor agreed. "I don't think that's what it's there for. It's how we make money. It ensures that we can keep franchisees profitable and provide them with new innovations on the cutting edge of technology." Finally, another franchisor flatly stated that he didn't want to monitor. "I don't want to be a policeman," he stated.

On this point, most franchisees agreed with franchisors:

"It's how they make money, it's their income."

"Basically it's running corp., it keeps people at corp. working with high quality."

"I don't look at it that way. That's one way of looking at it, but basically it's their income or rewards for their efforts."

"It's a moot point to me. It probably is a payment for their building, for the investment they have."

"I don't think the money is there to police or monitor us. It's there to assist us."

"There's nothing wrong with that, but I pay for advice."

Franchisees and franchisors agree that the royalty is a "right" of the company, the price for their expertise, and assumed to be an operating expense for franchisees. But a royalty is not paid in exchange for monitoring the system, as economists have stated. This is not to say that monitoring is not important, nor would franchise participants argue that monitoring is not an obligation of the franchisor. On the contrary, franchisors and franchisees believe that the system has to be monitored and that the franchisor has to carry out that task, but franchisors do not monitor because of the royalty.

"So what are franchisees getting when they pay the royalty?" I asked Mark Spinelli of Star Muffler.

"We have an obligation to monitor the system," he stated, "but the royalty is also for the development of our program. It's a rent, a license to continue operating."

"But it's a constant, right? It's a flat rate, so the top-revenue franchisees are paying—"

"—a lot," Spinelli broke in. "We know that the top guy, Pete Morgan, is not ever going to get the full value of what he pays us in terms of advice. He's paying over $150,000 a year, and that is way too much for advice. But he's not paying just for advice. He's paying for the use of the name, for the on-going support, for the license, and we think it's a fair price."

"No matter how much value you think you're getting," stated a high-revenue King Cleaners franchisee, "it's hard to write out that check. You forget the beginning, and you come to think of the franchise as being yours. It's easy to think, 'Hey, I built this thing myself, King Cleaners did nothing for me, and now that I'm making a lot of money they want a big chunk of cash.' But that's the wrong way to think of it. If you think of it that way, you'll be angry all the time, thinking, 'I'm getting ripped off by the company.' You have to remember the beginning, and you have to think of it as a right to continue operating under the trademark. Otherwise, you might as well quit and do something else."

## LONG-TERM CONTRACT, SHORT-TERM SURVIVAL

Franchise systems are contractual systems, and each and every franchise company has an explicit contract or "franchise agreement" that provides operational guidelines to franchisees. The franchise agreement may detail such issues as the boundaries, obligations, fee schedule, operating procedures, and financial arrangements of both parties. Of course, the agreement governs both parties in the event that they deviate from the contract. In addition to a franchise agreement, companies must also file with the Federal Trade Commission a document called the Uniform Franchise Offering Circular (UFOC), which provides public information on many aspects of the franchise system, including number of franchise units, all associated costs to franchisees, litigation history (over the past ten years) of the principals, expected earnings and profits (optional), and a wide range of obligations, financial arrangements, trademark rights, and so forth. For the savvy, research-oriented franchisee, there is ample opportunity to gain a robust picture of the franchisor, yet few franchisees bother with this.

"Did you look over the UFOC before deciding on this franchise?" I asked a franchisee at King Cleaners.

"Nah," he responded.

"How about the contract?"

"Yeah, I looked over the contract. I read the whole thing myself."

"You didn't use a lawyer?" I was surprised, because contracts can easily be a hundred pages or more.

"No. I didn't have a lawyer. I read all that stuff myself. Why use a lawyer? Corp's not gonna alter it anyway."

Most likely, he's right, for contracts are presented to franchisees as take-it-or-leave-it documents. In part, contracts are presented this way because franchisors wish to keep the system "pure," keep the standards high, establish a consistent trademark, and ease administrative tasks that would surely accompany a multitude of contracts. Writing separate contracts for the tens, hundreds, or thousands of franchisees would be cumbersome and not all that efficient. But it is also true that both franchisors and franchisees believe themselves to be business people, not lawyers, and their main goal is to get a franchise unit up and operational in short order. A contract, or more precisely, a negotiated contract is a hindrance to that goal. Finally, there is a general belief held by franchisors and franchisees that a contract is not indicative of how the business is operated by the franchisor.

Indeed, contracts can never be a surrogate for experience. Even with full disclosure, franchisees are likely to echo the sentiment expressed by a franchisee at a trade association meeting, "No matter how much due diligence a new franchisee does prior to entering into an agreement, he or she cannot possibly know anything like a complete picture of the business systems of the franchisor. Only after he or she enters into the agreement and has a few years under the belt can they really understand how the system works. No amount of disclosure can ever take the place of hands-on experience, and that takes time."

Because franchisors write the terms of their franchise agreements, it comes as no surprise that the agreement is slanted in their favor. But lately, franchise attorneys such as Rupert Barkoff have noted that the obligations of franchisees have increased greatly and become more onerous. According to Barkoff, franchise agreements are triple the size of a few years ago and include listings of twenty or more events that could lead to termination in addition to "good cause." They require the franchisee to litigate or arbitrate disputes in the county where the franchisor has its principal place of business. They have clauses that prohibit the arbitrator from awarding punitive or consequential damages, and they place limitations on the franchisee family's ability to engage in competitive businesses, even when they have no direct involvement in the franchised business. In fact, as Barkoff states, "The list could go on endlessly."[3]

Although it appears that contracts are unfair to franchisees, franchisors also incur risks because they cannot anticipate changes in the market or, oftentimes, foresee opportunities. For instance, one of the franchisees at King Cleaners spoke about the higher royalty rate he had to pay.

"The residential market is more lucrative, so we pay a higher royalty," he explained.

"Is that viewed as a problem, do you think?" I asked.

"No, not really, especially for the guys that have a disaster damage franchise."

"Who are those guys?"

"They're the ones that go into a home after a fire, smoke damage, or a flood. Or, it could be some other natural disaster.

3. House Committee on Small Business, *Franchising in the U.S. Economy,* 101 Cong., 2d sess., 1990, 114–32.

We work a lot with insurance companies, so the customer never really cares about price. But even that business is changing, and the new franchisees are not going to make as much as the old guys."

"Why, are there fewer disasters?"

"I don't think so. It's not that. They've changed the contract and are taking away a significant source of income. See, when they first started this business, King Cleaners thought that franchisees in the residential markets could add this segment of the market to their current operations as an extra service. But a couple of the franchisees got really smart. They figured out that for nearly all of the disaster claims the house had to be completely emptied, so they started their own moving companies. Then they also built warehouses to hold the furniture. That was a huge source of income, and King Cleaners was cut out of all royalties on that. So they tried to get royalties on the moving and storage by saying, you know, 'This is all part of the license so you owe us the same royalty on the moving and storage income.' But the franchisees said, 'No way. We thought of this, this is a separate business that has nothing to do with King Cleaners. You guys are in the cleaning business, and this is moving and storage.' Well, they went to court over it and the court sided with the franchisees. So King Cleaners rewrote the contract, and now the new guys have to pay royalties on moving and storage income."

King Cleaners is in the fortunate position of being able to rewrite the contract since their contract runs five years, a rather short time span in franchising circles. Perhaps having a five-year contract is one lesson the company learned from being a franchisor for the past half-century. Star Muffler and Sign Masters have the more typical twenty-year contract, and a change in terms would certainly be more difficult to institute.

The long-term nature of contracts is one of the defining characteristics of franchising, and it is an aspect of the strategy that appears to serve franchisors and franchisees well. For franchisees, a long-term contract means that all effort expended toward building the local market, increasing the value of the brand, and building goodwill in the community can reap returns in the future.

I once asked Mark Spinelli of Star Muffler why they had such a long-term contract, and he replied, "Nobody would want to buy a franchise in this industry with anything less than a twenty-year guarantee, and I respect that. The economics of this industry do not support anything less. I suppose we could go down to fifteen years, and we have thought about that, but anything less would not be fair to franchisees." From a franchisor's perspective, a long-term contract provides some semblance of stability, but not much.

In fact, it is a trap to think of a long-term agreement, say, a twenty-year contract, as evidence that franchise systems are relatively stable. This fiction is now being addressed by academics and people within the industry. For instance, a major industry trade association stated that in 1989 "less than 3 percent of business format franchisee-owned outlets were discontinued— many for reasons other than business failure" and that "65 percent of business start-ups fail within five years."[4] Today, the association takes a much more conservative approach to franchise success. An executive with the organization confided to me, "We are not aware of any current studies that compare survival rates and have doubts that this could be done since data on franchising are so hard to obtain."

Nevertheless, research by Scott Shane provides new evidence that franchise failures were far more common than what the International Franchise Association had claimed. Shane analyzed the survivability of franchise systems in a wide range of industries from 1983 to 1993 and found that rather than a 95 percent success rate only about 25 percent survived.[5]

How can these numbers diverge as much as they appear to? Most likely the answer lies in how one defines "success" or

4. International Franchise Association, *Franchise Opportunities Guide* (Washington, D.C.: International Franchise Association, 1995), 28.

5. Scott A. Shane, "Hybrid Organizational Arrangements and Their Implications for Firm Growth and Survival: A Study of New Franchisors," *Academy of Management Journal* 39, no. 1 (1996): 232.

"survival." Most franchise companies measure the number of franchise units that survive from year to year rather than franchisees who survive from year to year. This measure understates some of the turbulence in the system, since it is quite possible that franchisees fail while franchise units survive. If one measures franchise success in terms of franchisees that survive from year to year, the numbers may differ significantly.

The turbulence, reflecting franchisee survival, is evident at the companies I studied. A year after I completed my research, I revisited King Cleaners, Sign Masters, and Star Muffler and asked them to indicate which franchisees were still in the system, which had left, and why. The results reflected the conclusions drawn from Shane's research. At King Cleaners the failure rate was more than 35 percent, at Sign Masters it was slightly above 24 percent, and at Star Muffler it was 9 percent. The failure rate at Star Muffler, while comparatively low, was over three times higher than what the International Franchise Association claimed, but significantly lower than what Shane found. I used the term "failure rate" because when I asked what happened to the franchisees that exited the system, I was given the cryptic response, "They're not here." I also asked other franchisees in the system what happened, and the typical response was more direct.

"What happened to some of the people on this list?" I asked George and Doug.

"They're out of business," replied George.

"What does that mean, does it mean they failed?"

"Nobody likes the term 'failure,'" said Doug. "They're out of business."

"Well, I don't mind the term failure—"

"—is that what you want to hear, that they failed?" asked Doug.

"No, I don't want to hear that if it's not true," I replied.

"OK, well, they're not here anymore, they couldn't make it," he said.

"That's what I needed to know," I said.

"Well, in your terms, yeah, I guess you could call it a failure, but we don't like to think of it that way. They tried their hardest, they gave it all they had, and they didn't make it," explained Doug.

"And the company sold more franchises in their place," said George. "There's a whole new bunch of guys in there, and we don't even think about the people who have come and gone since we started."

"We're the old-timers now," Doug interrupted. "We've been here all of five years, and we're two of the most experienced franchisees they've got."

I measured franchisee turnover a year after completing my research, so the "failure rate," if one wants to call it that, likewise describes the fluctuations and turnover for only one year. But in a short time, say, two or three years, each company could conceivably have a small core of franchisees like Doug and George, who understand the business well and contribute a large proportion of the revenues, and a much larger group of relatively new franchisees. Clearly, long-term contracts do not indicate the underlying stability of franchising. Although franchisors and franchisees may both prefer long-term contracts, franchisee tenure may be significantly shorter.

An analysis of contracts can take one only so far in understanding the dynamics of franchising. They are a necessary part of franchising, and although they set the tone for a system, contracts do not control the day-to-day behavior of franchisors or franchisees. Many franchisees sign the contract, file it away, and never give it a second thought until they decide to sell their unit or until some contractual issue emerges. As business people, franchisors and franchisees are much more likely to focus on other aspects of the franchise system, especially the day-to-day operations of the business. The short-lived tenure of franchisees is certainly due to something other than contracts, trademarks, and royalties.

# CHAPTER 3

KING CLEANERS

Larry drove his van into the parking lot where I was standing. "You're in luck today," he declared.

"I'm in luck?" I repeated as I hopped in the van.

"Yeah, I mean, you're lucky we have a place to go to today. I have an important client that we have to go to first and, to tell you the truth, earlier today I didn't think I'd have this client at all."

"Why's that?"

"Well, I got a call at seven this morning from the contract manager over there, and he says to me, 'Larry, this is, you know, the manager from so-and-so. You're terminated.' I mean, that was the first thing he said, not 'Hello' or anything. He just said, 'You're terminated.' Nice way to wake up! And so I asked the guy, 'What do you mean we're terminated? What's going on?' And at first he wouldn't tell me, he just said that things weren't working out, that there had been a few complaints, and that he was sorry but that he was going to have to let me go. Well, I figure that he's just being a heavy, a tough guy, because if he were really unhappy he wouldn't even call, he'd just send a letter. Most people just send a letter that says, you know, 'You're terminated, effective immediately.'"

"Really? People terminate you without any warning, with just a letter?"

"Oh, yeah, it happens all the time. So anyway, I figured that he's getting heat from somebody, probably the secretaries, to get rid of us. So I say to the guy, 'Wait a minute, hold on there, let me come down and straighten this thing out.' And so I went down there and met with the guy and he showed me some things, really minor things like the coffee cups weren't spotless, stuff like that. Well, he decided to give me a second chance, but he told me, you know, 'One more slip-up and you're through. That's it.' So that's where we're going first. I just hope my guys show up. And really, I feel kinda bad for them. They take the bus from the projects in Chicago, and it takes them about an hour and a half to get there. One of the guys has like, I don't know, something like five kids."

"Is this their only job?"

"Yeah. So if I lose this account that's it for them."

As we made our way toward the client site, I looked around Larry's van. It was in pretty bad shape. Somewhat rusted on the outside, it lacked any evidence that it was a King Cleaners van. It did not sport the company logo and was a dull gray rather than the traditional company colors. Inside, various chemicals and equipment were strewn about in haphazard fashion, and as we jolted down the side streets of one of Chicago's industrial parks, everything became even more of a jumbled mess.

"It looks like you've gotten a lot of use out of this van," I ventured.

"Yeah," he replied, "John (the franchisor) has been getting on my case to, you know, paint the van with the right colors and put the logo on. He even gave me the name of a guy who'll paint it for a couple hundred bucks, but I don't know. I mean, I've got over two hundred thousand miles on it, and it's on the second engine. And it's only three years old! I just don't think it makes sense to put any money into this van right now. This is a really important account for me right now, and if I lose it I'll be in big trouble so I don't want to put anything in to the van yet. I just lost another account a couple of days ago, and that hurts."

"Oh yeah? Was that a big account?"

"It was for me," he said. "I've been cleaning some park district buildings for the past two years, and they use a competitive bid system. I made a bid this year on the buildings of $45,000, but they gave it to a guy who had a bid of $44,820. That works out to be $15 per month less than my bid. I couldn't believe I lost the bid because I've never received any complaints or anything. I talked to the city manager about it, you know, to find out whether they were unsatisfied with my work or how this came about, and he said that they didn't have any problems with my work. They just have to go with the lowest bidder. So I lost a $45,000 account over $15 a month. I don't know, it seems like a pretty small amount to lose out on a contract," he concluded resignedly.

Larry was in his late thirties and had been operating his franchise for five years. His longevity in franchising belied the turbulence he faced and the hard work he put into his business. Like many franchisees at King Cleaners, Larry carried out multiple tasks, and on this particular day he was working in operations so he looked more like a maintenance worker than a franchise business manager.

When asked why he bought a franchise he said, "Well, I had been working a bunch of jobs that had no real potential. I was a manager at a video game arcade, I sold wine, and I was an assistant manager at a drug store. You know, those jobs wouldn't lead to anything. I thought this would be something I could grow." But, like countless other King Cleaners franchisees, he still faced a battle in keeping his franchise unit solvent. The fact that Larry struggles at all in his franchise unit seems surprising, especially since King Cleaners is one of the leading franchise companies in the world.

CORPORATE

From an inauspicious start as a moth-cleaning business in 1928, King Cleaners has grown into a global corporation with thousands of franchisees and revenues in the billions of dollars. King Cleaners has expanded into residential carpet and window cleaning as well as into light household cleaning. The company also broadened into the commercial sector, offering building maintenance and janitorial work. This expansion began on a national scale in the early 1950s, first through branch operations and then through franchising. Wayne Franklin, founder of King Cleaners, explained that he used the franchise strategy because he wanted to give people the opportunity to own their own business and that he initially offered a distributorship to his existing managers. According to one of the original distributors, however, the reason King Cleaners began franchising had less to do with providing people the opportunity to own a business and more to do with finances.

"Why do you think the company began to franchise?" I asked.

"Why did they franchise!" he repeated. "Because it was the only way they could make money. When we first started to expand in the early 1950s, we started a branch office in New Jersey somewhere, but they could never figure out how to run the thing. Franklin used to say that they franchised because he wanted to give the working man, the common guy, the opportunity to own and operate his own business. But to my knowledge, he franchised because he couldn't figure out any other way to make money."

"I see. Why does the company make more money franchising?"

He thought for a moment before answering. "I think they make out better franchising because they spread the risk over a wider area and the fluctuations in the market are absorbed by the franchisee and only partially by the company. See, since King Cleaners only makes, let's say, 10 percent of gross sales, any wild changes in the market are smoothed over in their earnings. If the market goes bad in Atlanta, it might be great in New York. That's bad for the Atlanta franchisees, but not so bad for King Cleaners. They're not out much."

Not only does King Cleaners avoid the full impact of fluctuations in the market, but by franchising they also avoid some of the thornier issues that plague nonfranchised companies. For instance, I once asked Doug about something I had witnessed in another franchisee's operation.

"Do you think that Corporate should be able to tell you how to run your business?" I asked.

"Absolutely not!" he exclaimed. "I can run it in any fashion I want."

"But I saw some guys out there in your company who are doing terrible things. One guy treated his employees in a brutal way."

"Well, what do you think Corporate would do if an employee called and said, 'So-and-so is hitting me'?"

"I know what they should do," I replied.

"What should they do?" Doug asked in a confrontational tone.

"They should reprimand him, or take some sort of action that—"

"That's what they *should* do, but they won't. If something like that comes up, they'll wipe their hands clean of the whole mess. That's why they franchise, so they won't have to deal with problems like that. Corporate hardly considers me to be a part of the company; why would they think of my employees as part of the company? You know that all of our workers are hourly folks, they're all part-time workers, and a lot of them come from pretty poor backgrounds. There are all sorts of things that happen on a daily basis that Corporate doesn't know about and doesn't want to know about. They only want the royalty."

Franklin's strategy to collect a royalty through franchising proved to be profitable, but a fortuitous turn of events also helped the company. When King Cleaners first began to offer services for commercial clients in the 1950s, it was a small company that lacked capital assets. In particular, it did not have a factory to clean carpets. Instead, the company provided cleaning services "on location" at the client site.

Although common today, at the time it was a novel strategy. Industry mainstays owned cleaning factories and would send a crew to pick up a carpet, which would be cleaned at the factory and then returned a week later. But once wall-to-wall carpet became commonplace in houses and businesses, the cleaning factory became a liability. King Cleaners found itself uniquely positioned to take full advantage of the emerging commercial and residential markets.

Today King Cleaners is the leader in what is a very large industry. In fact, commercial cleaning services—building maintenance and janitorial work—are typically billed out at one dollar per square foot per year, so a large metropolitan market can be worth well over $80 billion a year.

Despite the Fortune 500 ranking, international presence, and long-term commitment to franchising, King Cleaners is not a household name. At one of the annual meetings of franchisees I attended, a vice president shared the results of a recent marketing survey. It asked a simple question: "What companies come to mind when you think of cleaning services?" Yet a whopping 81 percent of the respondents could not name *any* company in the cleaning business. Even after respondents were given a list of companies in the industry, only 30 percent recognized King Cleaners as a provider of cleaning services. So the King Cleaners franchisee toils in relative obscurity selling what is in large part a generic service that for many commercial clients is not a particularly high priority. In fact, one senior executive declared, "A company will spend millions of dollars to construct a new building, but will give little thought on how to maintain it. So, for example, they'll put in a marble floor entrance, which looks terrific when it's new, but is absolutely terrible to clean. You can't really make it look nice and it's slippery in the winter, it's slick after a rain, it shows dirt and mud easily. So the first thing people see when they enter a new building is a dirty floor, and they'll blame us for it."

ON THIN ICE

As we rode along in the van making our way to the important client, Larry said, "Here, I got a uniform for you." He handed me nothing more that a T-shirt with the King Cleaners logo on it.

"Thanks. So what do you want me to do here?"

"Well, are you sure you want to work with the guys? I mean, it's just cleaning."

"Yeah, you bet. That's a big part of my research approach, working in the frontline operations of franchise units."

"I see. Well, I can sure use the free help. OK, then. I'll drop you off with my guys, and you can work with them for awhile.

Then I'll stop by to pick you up later, and you can visit some of the other sites."

We arrived at the client site located in an industrial park on Chicago's Southwest Side in a multiethnic, working-class neighborhood. The company, which had about two hundred employees, manufactured metal fasteners, strapping, and other assorted products such as ceiling tiles. The site consisted of two buildings separated by a small parking lot, and the larger and newer building had two floors of office space in the front where the sales, marketing, and administrative personnel worked. The back door of the office opened directly into a large warehouse and loading dock. The other building was older and slightly smaller but organized in the same way. A large entryway off the parking lot led to the manufacturing processes and shop floor, while the front part of the building contained the offices of the chief executive officer and vice presidents as well as two conference rooms. Larry's contract called for him to clean the executive and administrative offices in each building. All other cleaning and maintenance outside of the building (the parking lot, lawn, and exterior) as well as the manufacturing and loading dock areas were the responsibility of the company's maintenance staff.

We entered the site through the loading dock, and as we made our way to the administrative offices, Larry ran into one of the maintenance workers from the company.

"So," he laughed, "I hear that the ladies are giving you a hard time."

"Yeah, I guess so," said Larry.

"Well, they're pretty tough. It isn't the first time they've given someone a hard time. But, hey, at least you're getting a second chance."

"Yeah," Larry agreed, "we'll see how it goes."

After the worker left, I asked Larry, "Does he compete with you?"

"That guy? No, I don't think so. This is kinda a funny contract. I don't know why they do it this way, but they don't want that guy in the main offices. They don't want anybody from the loading docks in the main building, in the office part. So they hire a guy like me to take care of that part."

We waited for Larry's two employees to arrive, but when the office workers left at 5 P.M., we headed in to start cleaning. Since it was my first day on the job, I figured I would receive some training, but Larry just handed me a dust rag and a bottle of spray and said, "You know how to dust, don't you? Just make sure that you leave everything on the desk the way it is. People get really angry if you move things on their desk to clean." I started out cleaning the executive offices, and Larry's two workers showed up a few minutes later. They were African Americans in their mid-twenties who lived on the South Side. Larry started one worker in the kitchen area and especially emphasized to the employee the importance of cleaning the coffee mugs.

"That's another funny thing about this contract," Larry told me. "They really don't seem to care about anything except the coffee mugs. They never complain about their desks, the floors, or the carpets. But if the women's bathroom has one spot on the mirror or if one coffee mug is dirty, they scream." He interrupted himself to yell, "Hey, Ted, make sure the kitchen area is really clean, otherwise we won't have a job here."

"I cleaned 'em," Ted answered back. "I always clean 'em."

"Well, yeah, I know, but somebody came in here after we left and probably had a cup of coffee or something. Messed it up after we left."

Larry turned to me. "We can't stop a problem like that."

While Ted cleaned the kitchen, the other worker, David, started to vacuum. The vacuum used by franchisees is radically different in design and function from an ordinary vacuum. The vacuum is far more powerful than a household vacuum and is also relatively light—about twenty pounds—so that a wide range of people can operate it. The vacuum is cylindrical-shaped like an air tank used in scuba diving, but the intake is large in diameter and the cord is two hundred feet long. The worker straps the vacuum onto his or her back and then walks as quickly as possible along the high-traffic areas of an office vacuuming up only the particles, paper clips, staples, and other objects that are immediately visible. Any specks or dirt that are not big enough to be easily seen are passed over. So the corners of rooms, the edges of a hallway, and carpet underneath tables and desks are not cleaned. Although the areas are not "clean" by most standards, this service, called a "spot-vac" contract, is typical for most businesses and allows an average worker to clean an eight thousand square foot building in about one half of an hour.

I asked Larry, "What about these spots on the carpet? Do you want us to clean them?"

"No, we have to sell a special cleaning service to get those spots, and it's usually pretty hard to do. Some guys expect you to do it for free, they think that that's part of the contract. But we sell it as a special service."

As we finished with the first floor and made our way to the second, Larry's wife, Liz, and two-year-old daughter arrived.

"Couldn't you get your mother to watch her?" Larry asked.

"No," she responded.

. "Well, I guess it will be OK."

Larry turned to me. "Usually she doesn't clean; she does the book work, but this is a really important account for me and if I lose it, I'll be in trouble."

Liz began to dust, and their daughter followed her around, climbing on chairs and exploring parts of the office. On the second floor, Larry pointed out the contract manager's office.

"This is the manager's office. We need to make sure that this is really clean."

Larry left to check on other clients and returned sometime after midnight to double-check our progress. By then, we were in the smaller building finishing up on one of the conference rooms. While passing through an area where secretaries work, Larry stopped to tidy up and found a paper clip under one desk.

"Aha!" he exclaimed, "The old paper clip trick!"

"What's that?" I asked.

"Oh, some people place a paper clip there on purpose so that later they can say, you know, 'I had a paper clip under my desk for three days, and you guys never cleaned under there.' It's a common trick. Or sometimes they'll point out an orange spot on the floor. You know, something that's probably been there longer than they have. But they do things like that just to get you."

"Aren't you being paranoid?"

"Hey, it happens. These women are vicious. I know that they are the only ones complaining about anything. The other night I came back at about 10:30 P.M. just to make a final check, and I found their bathroom was really dirty. It had been cleaned—I cleaned it myself—but some worker from the shop floor came in and used it. He had greasy feet, you know, and it looked like we had never been there. I was really lucky to catch that. There's no way that we can avoid a problem like that. If people come in and use the bathroom with dirty feet after we clean, there's not much we can do. I even mentioned it to the contract manager, and he just shrugged it off, he just laughed and said that he has to keep the women happy. So, I don't know."

"Keeping the women happy" is one of the most important tasks franchisees face. While working with one of the top franchisees, Rusty, I learned how he avoided the problems Larry had encountered.

"Are there differences between men and women in how they view cleaning services?" I asked.

"Oh yeah, man," said Rusty, "women in organizations cause by far the greatest problems. Women think of the office as their home away from home, and they expect it to be spotless. You really have to manage that if you want to survive."

"Well, what do you do?"

"Me? I set the expectations right at the beginning of the contract. I don't even do a day's work before calling a meeting of the people at the client site. I gather all the people together, mostly the secretaries, and I say something like, 'Ladies, we're your new cleaning service, and this is what we do. We will spot vacuum the carpet every day and that means that we only clean those spots in the most commonly walked places and only those specks that are visible. If you spill your coffee on the carpet, we won't clean it up. We will not clean your desk if there is anything on it. We will clean it once a week if you clear it. If you all want to get together and decide on a particular day, say, Friday, we can then clean all of them on that day. We will do a thorough cleaning once a month, vacuuming everywhere. If there are things on the carpet after that cleaning, then you have a legitimate gripe. Now, if you don't like the structure of this deal, talk to your boss, because this is what you're paying for.'"

"Does that work?"

"Sure does. If you don't do that, you won't last two weeks with any corporate client."

"Well, if franchisees are trained to manage accounts properly I don't see why—"

"Trained!" he shouted. "Corporate doesn't train us to manage that way. Corporate tells us to manage the contract manager, but that's only a small part of it. No, I figured that out myself."

"Here," he reached behind his desk and pulled out the King Cleaners training manual. "This is the type of training we get. Take a look at this sage advice." He showed me a page as he read the manual. "Do not fail to wear a coat and tie! We have heard all the excuses for not wearing a coat and tie; however, the coat and tie is still the most widely recognized symbol of a businessman. This will set you apart from 99 percent of the other janitors who are in the business. We are professionals, so let us dress like professionals!'"

"That's the level we're dealing with here!" snorted Rusty. "And the sad thing is, a lot of the franchisees need to be told to wear a coat and tie. Just the other day I went to a corporate account that was open for bidding, and there were probably twelve different guys there. I was the only one wearing a suit and one guy," he chuckled. "One guy showed up with a bucket and mop! Can you believe that? We're talking about a several hundred thousand dollar contract here, and he shows up like he's going to do the work himself!" Rusty laughed again but then became serious and said, "But if you want to keep your accounts running smoothly, you have to manage the women. Absolutely have to."

FINAL DAYS

A few days after the cleaning at the metal fastener company site in which I participated, Larry put together a special weekend crew to provide a thorough cleaning of it. We buffed and waxed the floors, cleaned the entire carpet, polished the desks, and had the site looking first-rate. Larry provided all these services at his own expense since it was not part of his contract. Yet later that week, Larry was terminated.

"Yeah," Larry said, "The contract manager called and said, 'That's it. You're through.' And then hung up the phone."

"Did you know who it was?"

"Oh yeah. I recognized him. So I called him back and said, 'I thought we had straightened everything out,' and he said, 'It's not the quality of the service. We had some adding machines stolen last night.' I mean, he was really angry about it. There was no way I was going to be able to convince him to give me another chance. So I've got to go over there before my guys get there and tell them they're through."

"How do you think they'll take that news?"

"Not very good. One of them has, like, six kids, and this is his only job. I really like him—he's a nice guy and I'd like to try to do something for both of them, but I don't have enough work right now."

"They're accused of stealing adding machines?"

"Yeah, can you believe that? That's what I said! But, I mean they're gone. The guy took me to the office where they were stolen, and he's right. I mean, they used to be there and now they're not. To tell you the truth, I don't think those guys stole an adding machine. They're really big, heavy machines, and these guys have to ride the bus back to the projects. I just don't think they'd do it. They have to walk out past the loading dock, a half-mile down the street, wait for the bus—and all of this after midnight. And, in this neighborhood, I mean, they'd never make it. I'm sure some cop would stop them if he saw them hauling an adding machine around the neighborhood after midnight. I mean, geez! And there are people around here working the night shift. Why would they steal it? A computer or calculator makes sense, but an adding machine is worth almost nothing. I mean, who uses adding machines? So I lost the contract, and I have to buy the guy four hundred dollars worth of adding machines."

He reflected for a moment. "Blacks worry a lot of clients. I had one guy who called and told me that an expensive calculator had been stolen by my worker from some executive offices, even though no one saw her take it. But I know my worker real well, and she wouldn't take anything. She had to clean these executive offices that they kept locked, and she would get a key from a drawer in the secretary's desk, unlock the offices, and then replace the key when she was done. I asked her if she could have left the key somewhere, and she said that she didn't do that, that she always did it the same way. Anyway, about two days later, the guy calls back and says they found the calculator because someone had borrowed it and then forgotten to take it back. Well, I tell you, that's rare. I mean, most guys would never have admitted that, they'd just terminate you. If you got blacks cleaning a building, it gives the workers a license to go in there and steal things."

To be sure, the race of employees can impact franchise operations. The far more critical issue, however, is not the race of employees but the fact that cleaning tasks require few skills of frontline workers. The low skill required of workers means that the pool of applicants contains some of the least educated and most poorly motivated workers in the economy, and problems of absenteeism and turnover abound. One franchisee told me, "If an employee just shows up to work, they're great, and if they actually do some work, well, they would be one of the very best employees I have." Another franchisee stated, in all seriousness, "For every one hundred people I hire, I keep six."

Of course, it is also the case that employees are likely to exit voluntarily. At wages of $4.50 (at the time, the minimum) to $7.00 per hour, it is no wonder that employees are wage-sensitive. As one franchisee said, "My employees are not very loyal. I mean, these guys will change jobs for ten cents an hour.

I tell 'em, 'you're going to lose money by changing jobs,' but they still change." They also change jobs because King Cleaners franchisees hire only part-time workers and offer no benefits or overtime. Commented one franchisee, "I don't like it, but I can't afford to do it any other way. I got a guy who works sixty hours a week, but he's still part-time."

"How do you do that?"

"Well, I just treat each client as a separate account and make sure that he spends time at each client site. He's a great worker, but he's always a part-time worker."

Besides high turnover and absenteeism rates among their employees, franchisees face a difficult task in managing workers because many are minorities with a limited command of English. King Cleaners provides a training video that explains, mainly through the use of different colored bottles and containers, which products should be used in particular applications.

Managing frontline workers also involves communicating to employees various changes in the operating procedures, figuring out the logistics of who works where and how they will make it to the next job site, and trusting them to work on their own in office sites and make the right decisions. These problems are compounded for the franchisee that relies upon a multiethnic workforce. "I'd be out of business if I didn't have a bilingual supervisor," stated one franchisee.

Yet others seem to manage with no interpreter at all. I asked one such franchisee, "Does that make you nervous, to not be able to communicate with your employees?"

"Oh, yeah, really nervous. But I can't find anyone who speaks Spanish. I do have a couple of guys that I trust to lock up, and so far I haven't had any problems."

Finding people to trust is not only taxing, but in franchises like King Cleaners it is also extremely critical because franchisees are not directly supervising employees. Job sites are located in disparate locations, workers at larger client sites are spread out across several floors or buildings, and work takes place in the evening and in the late-night hours. The ability of franchisees to monitor employees, even during a spot check, is limited.

Franchising may afford people with the opportunity to operate their own business, but at King Cleaners they often do so on the fringes of the economy, providing a service that is generic and therefore vulnerable to price competition. In this precarious position, franchisee operations act as shock absorbers for the corporation. Franchisees absorb the fluctuations in the economy, shelter the company from a largely temporary underclass of workers, and oversee and manage what is largely a noncritical service for small- to mid-size clients. It was not all that surprising to me to hear Larry, after a worker accidentally spilled coffee grounds on the floor and whisked them away rather than clean them up, comment, "Good, that's a good idea." For the King Cleaners franchisee, any shortcut helps.

# CHAPTER 4

SIGN MASTERS

"I'm disenchanted with franchising as a method of business," sighed Victor, one of the most successful franchisees at Sign Masters. It was about 10 P.M. on a weeknight, and Victor and his wife, Marge, still had several hours of work to complete before closing their shop.

"Why is that?" I asked. "Because of what happened earlier today?"

"What was that?"

"You know, the guy who walked in, asked if this was a franchise, and then when he found out it was, turned around and walked out."

"Oh, that guy. No, that's not it. That wasn't the first time someone has come in here, asked if we were a franchise, and then walked out. A couple of years ago I would have been baffled by something like that, but now it makes perfect sense. I've come to learn that for certain customers there is a stigma attached to being a franchise. Who knows? Maybe that guy used to be a franchisee. No, I guess I'm disenchanted with franchising because it differs from what I expected. And I really did my homework before buying a franchise. I thought I was making a very sound decision by coming into this business."

"What kind of homework did you do?"

"I had a golden parachute, and I was thinking that I had two options: try to get another corporate job, or start something on my own. Then I read an article in the *Wall Street Journal* that featured the computerized sign industry, and it also mentioned something about the higher success rate of franchising—the success rate was way higher, something on the order of 95 percent—so I went to a franchise expo to explore the possibility. I probably spent three months looking at nearly every franchise opportunity that fit my criteria. I knew this was a big decision. I also knew absolutely nothing about franchising, so I took my time. I literally looked at forty-four different opportunities.

"I liked Stu Beyer," he continued, "and the fact that this was a young industry with high growth potential. Compared to other franchise systems, I thought this one would fit me better. Most of the franchise concepts out there are unattractive businesses, like mufflers, fast-food restaurants, or convenience stores. I didn't like the people selling those franchises, and I didn't like the business. Here, you get to use cutting-edge technology with a computer. It's clean work, and our clients are other business people—people that I understand. But now, I don't know. . . ."

Then he announced, "I still like Stu Beyer. I think he is a great guy, but he's in way over his head and he's done some things that really anger me."

"What types of things? I thought everything was covered in the contract."

Victor stopped cutting vinyl and said, "Sure, the basic things are covered in the contract, but I'm talking about the things that make a business a success. We used to have communication downstream. Now the franchisor is silent. Did you hear what happened at the last franchisee meeting?"

"No, I didn't."

"Oh, well, we had our annual meeting, and Beyer didn't show up! He avoided us completely. I want to know about the financials and what he's doing to grow the business and improve services. He avoided the issue entirely and didn't even show his face at the meeting! It's unbelievable to me that a CEO would act like that. Just unbelievable."

"Well, what do you think is going on?" I asked.

"I think he's losing his business. We've heard rumors that he has his house up for sale, and airplane. You knew that he flew in Vietnam?"

"No, I didn't know that."

"Yeah, he flew in 'Nam and had some sort of military airplane. That's up for sale, too. Anyway, if you'd come here six months ago, I would have thought we wouldn't be here now. I would be here, I'll survive, but I would have thought that the company would be gone."

"Why do you think that is?"

"I don't know. I think he's bringing in the wrong types of people here. He's bringing in a lot of people who bought into the technology, who love the technology. They may be great sign makers and, you know, it's a lot of fun making signs. I love making signs, but I have a business to run. Most of these new franchisees don't know much about business, and they seem to be happy breaking even. We need people who will grow the business."

Victor and Marge were in a relatively good position and would probably survive no matter what happened to the franchisor. But other franchisees were not so fortunate, and there was an anxiety that permeated Sign Masters as franchisees faced the real possibility that the entire system would collapse. The troubles of Sign Masters are often pinned on Stu Beyer, the founder. Although he is partially to blame, Beyer is also a victim. In the end, he lost his business, house, and personal belongings trying to keep afloat a business idea that was so at odds with the environment that it probably could not have been saved, despite any effort.

ENTREPRENEUR

The corporate offices of Sign Masters were impressive, and were it not for my ethnographic work inside franchisee operations, I might have believed most of what Stu Beyer shared about his vision and company. Located in an upscale suburban office complex, the company occupied the entire fourth floor. The office was lavishly appointed and decorated with original art. An assistant greeted me as I exited the elevator and escorted me to a plush waiting area outside the executive suite. Stu Beyer was very friendly when I had met him several months earlier, and he was eager to receive an update on the progress of my work.

"There you are! Did you have any trouble finding the place?" he asked.

"No, I didn't. This is a very nice office."

"Thanks, we have been very successful so far, and we are one of the biggest computerized sign graphics companies in the United States."

"Really? I didn't know that."

"Oh, we're not that big compared to McDonald's," he laughed, "but we'll get there. We're in an emerging industry, and we were one of the first companies to franchise. I expect that the sign market will be one of the biggest markets by the year 2000. I think realistically that this industry will have ten thousand franchisees—and that's a conservative estimate. It's already a high-growth industry. It's got everything you could want—technology, creativity, and independence. I've done some studying on other industries, and I think we're very similar to the photocopy industry—you know, the quick copy places. They were a new industry in the 1970s and they had double-digit growth rates for twenty years. We'll be just like that—probably bigger."

In his mid-forties, Stu Beyer was an affable, dynamic, and genuine man. He was a consummate salesman, and while I came to believe that nearly all of his ideas about Sign Masters and his projections for the computerized sign industry were unrealistic, it was probably his optimism and enthusiasm that kept Sign Masters solvent for nearly ten years. Beyer had an interesting history. The son of a watchmaker, he attended junior college and earned an associate of arts degree in forestry but was drafted during the Vietnam War and abandoned his formal education. Upon his return to the United States, Stu worked in his father's jewelry store but soon tired of the limited possibilities. Instead, he purchased a lawn care franchise, moved over to the franchisor side of the business, and became president and then principal owner. In 1985, Beyer sold the company to a Fortune 500 company and used the proceeds to start Sign Masters. He never regretted the decision.

"I made some money on the sale of the franchise," he told me, "but I didn't want to work in the corporate offices of a large company. I've spent my whole career building companies, and I knew that working in that environment would kill me. I was also too young to retire, so I looked for a new challenge."

"But, of all the possible businesses to start, why did you start a sign business?"

"That's actually a funny story," he said. "One day I was in the mall down here, and I went into a store and asked the proprietor about a sign that caught my attention. I asked simple questions like where he got it, how the service was, things like that. Well, he had a long list of complaints about the expense, time, and quality of signage. You know, the signs were never done on time, they often came back from the shop wrong, and since the signs were hand painted, they were expensive. Well, that was pretty interesting to hear. I mean, that's a business problem screaming for a solution, so I went around to other business owners in the mall and they said the same thing! So I'm thinking, there is probably a niche here to make signs cheaper and more reliably. The other thing is, I became frustrated with customers in the lawn care business. If there was one thing I learned from that business, it was that Joe Homeowner is a fickle customer. Joe Homeowner is price-sensitive. In my lawn care franchise, I had customers I'd been providing services to for five years. Never had a complaint, never had problems in the service. But if a competitor offered a better price by five bucks, they'd jump ship. I didn't want to be in a business that had to sell to Joe Homeowner.

"But business people aren't like that. A business would rather cut off its arm than go find a new vender. Somewhere I read that 70 percent of consumers stop using a service because of an attitude of indifference on the part of the employee or owner, but 70 percent of businesses quit using a service because of lack of on-time delivery. This company addresses exactly that issue. We can deliver a sign to your exact specifications within twenty-four hours. That's right in our motto: 'The right sign, at the right price, right away . . . guaranteed!'"

"It sounds like you're on your way to another successful business."

"Thanks, I sure hope so."

"How has the franchising been going?"

"There's not anybody that knows franchising better than me, but I've had a heckuva time getting quality prospects," he stated. Beyer's enthusiasm waned, and he raised, for the first time, a concern. "I've been losing about forty thousand dollars per month, and I need to sell two franchises a month just to break even. It's actually a negative to be based here in the Midwest. Midwesterners are a 'B' market. Do you know what I mean by that?" he asked.

"No, not really."

"See, most of the good leads are either on the East Coast or the West Coast, but I can't get any of those people to move to the Midwest. I put an ad in *Entrepreneur* and expected three hundred leads, but I only got ninety leads and they were horrible leads. Absolutely horrible. I'm only selling one out of every seventy-five inquiries. And, well, you can do the math. It's not enough. Now I have my house and personal airplane up for sale, and until this thing gets straightened out, I am not taking any salary."

"Why do you have to franchise?"

"There are several reasons. We need the capital to expand, and it's better to expand with OPM—other people's money. But I believe in the concept. I always believed in the concept. Franchising is the fastest growing segment of the economy. Big corporations are downsizing! It's only franchising that is providing any real growth in the economy. Look what we've got: a great name, a great motto. We're on the cutting edge in operations. There isn't anybody that can do this better than me."

### INITIAL MISTAKES

Beyer's self-confidence as a franchisor was not shared by Sign Masters franchisees. "I like Stu Beyer," stated one franchisee, "He's a nice guy, but he doesn't know much about the business." Beyer's lack of business sense was evident in one of his early decisions on the location of franchise units. Originally, Beyer targeted small businesses as his best customers, so he located franchise units in industrial parks, where franchisees would be closer to clients and rental costs would be lower. But tucked away in an obscure corner of an industrial park these units floundered, and he later conceded that subsequent units would need to be located in strip malls. The relocation to prime real estate changed the cost structure of operating a franchise, not only in the basic monthly rent but also in the construction and design. No longer would a franchise unit be mostly a workshop; now it would be a storefront with higher associated costs of presentation quality for customers. However, once franchise units were located in strip malls, the customer base changed from mid-sized and small businesses to individual owners/operators of retail outlets.

"We really believed Stu Beyer when he said that this was a retail operation with relatively short hours and with business clients," stated one franchisee. "We thought that we'd be open from nine to five and then maybe work a little at night, but the hours are way more than that. We thought we'd be selling signs to companies like Sears and Motorola, but we're selling to other businesses like ourselves—people struggling to make ends meet. My customers are people in the strip mall, the bakery around the corner, and the woman who owns the flower shop. These people do not want to buy signs. Or if they do, they don't want to pay much for them."

"You need two, probably three people to operate this business," Victor explained to me. "One person has to be a good technician, someone with an artistic eye. Someone else needs to be out there making sales, and the third person has to be able to install signs. You could do it with fewer people, but you'd be working long, long hours and wouldn't be making much money."

"But do you need to be located in a strip mall?" I asked.

"We do get some traffic here because of our location, but it's not the type of customer we want—someone who comes in off the street is usually an individual business owner who needs one sign and that's it. Oh, there may be some follow-up work, but generally they need only one sign and it's usually a pretty small number by my standards. To really drive up sales, you can't wait for people to come in, you have to go out and make the sale. In that case, you don't need to be located here. There are no advantages."

A second mistake Beyer made had long-term consequences and was irrevocable: selling franchises to people with marginal qualifications. Current franchisees were perplexed by Beyer's inability to sell franchise units. "There seem to be so many people like me," stated one, "you know, middle management with cash. It seems like the market should be good to sell franchises. They [potential franchisees] have to be out there." But evidently not enough of them wanted a Sign Masters franchise, and as Beyer came under increased financial pressure he sold to anyone who had money and was willing to buy. These high-risk franchisees were people who either lacked business experience or people who lived in distant locations, or both. Because the new franchisees lacked business experience, corporate training and start-up costs skyrocketed. The fact that many of the franchisees were located far away from corporate headquarters also taxed Beyer's own ability to monitor their operations and use of the trademark.

Beyer's troubles in selling franchises were threefold. First, he sold the first twelve franchises to former franchisees from his lawn care business, so it was novel for him to sell to strangers. Second, competition in the industry heated up dramatically in the early 1990s, and the pool of high-quality franchisees shrank. One franchisee that began operations in 1989 told me, "I operated for two years without any competition, but now it seems that there is a sign shop—or two—in nearly every town."

Beyer's third and gravest mistake was to sell the flagship company store. This important decision would not only affect his revenues, but would later impair his ability to maintain credibility with franchisees. When he sold the company store, Beyer lost a profit center, a training center, a marketing testing program, and a laboratory. More important, without a company store Beyer was unable to effectively control the perception prospective franchisees have of the system. Instead, he had to rely on the goodwill of current franchisees to explain and sell the franchise system to them. He also left to chance the possibility that external factors might negatively influence the decision to purchase a franchise unit. For instance, with a company store Beyer could bring prospective franchisees to the shop at any time and thereby increase his chances of a successful sale. When is that opportune time? A franchisor at a pizza chain told me, "We never ask prospective franchisees to come by when it is convenient for them or at our own convenience. You're likely to get a prospect to show up at two in the afternoon. It's always quiet in the stores at two and that would be a great time to talk about the business. But we don't want that. We want a prospective franchisee to come by at six, when things are really busy because we want them to be turned on by the market, by the excitement of a dynamic business opportunity."

While a savvy franchisor will bring in prospective franchisees during the busiest time of the day, this is not a likely strategy for current franchisees. They would just as soon have prospective buyers stop by during slow periods. Without a company store, Beyer lost the ability to convey to prospective franchisees the excitement of a great business opportunity, and prospects were more likely to find a quiet and mostly boring franchise opportunity.

Moreover, without a company store Sign Masters was unable to train franchisees. "When we first started, we got so much help, but then we got nothing. Now when they come into the store they ask questions that make it seem like we're teaching them," stated one franchisee.

Another new franchisee lamented, "They never even properly demonstrated how to make a proper sign. I had no layouts of signs graphically, and I pretty much learned the business from a competitor. Basically, I'm self-taught."

Worse, Beyer had to again rely on the goodwill of franchisees close to headquarters to train new franchisees. "They come in here unannounced, and expect me to show new people how to do everything. I'm the closest one to Corporate so they pick on me, but I'm angry about it. I've talked to Beyer about it, but it doesn't do any good," stated one franchisee. Naturally, franchisees who train new ones have an opportunity to shape the perception newcomers will form of Stu Beyer and of Sign Masters.

The final casualty from losing the Sign Masters flagship store was a marked decrease in trustworthiness and credibility with franchisees. Because the company lost touch with changes in the market and customer needs, Beyer also lost the potential to understand firsthand the daily problems franchisees faced. "It's a lot of work, a ton of work to keep everything going," stated one franchisee angrily. "And I think they really don't have any idea how much time it takes to fill out all the reports they make us do. Really, it takes hours each week to fill out these pointless forms."

Another franchisee said despondently, "I have absolutely no free time of my own, and I resent it, terribly." Moreover, the top franchisee in the system commented in exasperation, "I don't understand why our volume is stuck at $200,000. I initially thought that $300,000, $400,000, or $500,000 should be obtainable, but we've been stuck for about a year." Unfortunately, Sign Masters was unable to give him any advice, and the highest-revenue franchisee operated in uncharted territory. He would have to concoct his own solutions if his business was to survive and flourish.

Stu Beyer sold the company store because of a financial crisis, but in doing so he lost far more than a revenue stream. His company lost the ability to market to potential franchisees or to train existing franchisees. Sign Masters did not have the capacity to bring in vendors who could improve and tailor products for franchisees. Most important, Sign Masters became a weaker company because the trust that franchisees once held in Stu Beyer had completely eroded. As Sign Masters moved farther away from the realities of the market, Beyer's credibility suffered, and he made a series of marketing blunders that further alienated franchisees from the company.

STRANGE BEDFELLOWS

The computerized sign graphics industry emerged during the mid-1980s shortly after personal computers became widely available and affordable. Stu Beyer was one of the first entrepreneurs to enter the sign business, but within a few years the market was increasingly saturated with competitors. In 1984, there was one company in the industry, and it had one franchised unit. By 1995, there were eighteen companies with more than 950 franchised units. The industry is populated today by companies with similar products, service, and strategies. Consequently, customers are price-sensitive.

The industry grew because personal computers became less expensive and computer-aided design (CAD) programs were widely distributed. Even so, the rapid increase in the industry over the last decade is perplexing to members of complimentary industries. An executive at a trade association for the electric and neon sign industry said to me, "We can't figure out why this business has increased so much. Who are these people? They've taken a really small segment of the market and have sold all these franchises, but they still can't be doing too well. Our industry is only $8 billion in sales a year, and I would guess that their numbers are much lower than that."

Increased competition forced Beyer to make some changes, one of which was refocusing on marketing programs. The results were not impressive. In one program, franchisees were "strongly encouraged" to purchase spools of yellow banners in anticipation of the return of soldiers from the Gulf War. This program was heavily endorsed by Stu Beyer because of his own experience as a Vietnam War veteran, but the yellow ribbon materials foisted upon franchisees turned into a marketing flop that never materialized, and franchisees were forced to absorb excess product. "That was a real fiasco," one franchisee said, "he [Beyer] thought people would rush to support the soldiers. But they didn't, and we got stuck with yellow ribbon. I still have it. Can't get rid of it. Do you want some?"

"No, thanks." I replied.

"Neither does anyone else."

Another company idea was to provide personalized bumper stickers for consumers. But at the "suggested" list price of fourteen dollars, few were sold. One franchisee lamented, "The people at Corporate don't know what customers need. Who's going to buy a fourteen-dollar bumper sticker? Even if I sell five a day, my profit margin is still only 2 percent. Do you know how many I'd have to sell to make it worth my while? I want a product that the customer needs, and I want high profit margins."

It is the solution to precisely that problem, discovering what customers want and selling it at high profit margins, that has eluded Sign Masters. Other questions hounded the company. Is this a retail business that should be located in high-rent locations or a production business that should be located in an industrial park? Are customers small business owners or large corporations? Are signs custom products or standard ones?

The answers are not clear-cut, and the lack of clarity led to all sorts of individual strategies by franchisees. One high-revenue franchisee said, "I don't want any ten dollar customers. You can ten and twenty dollar yourself to death." However, the small one-time customer most often buys a sign. As one franchisee aptly noted, "The sign business is goofy. Customers don't tell you if they like your product, and the only measure of success is the amount of repeat business, but a lot of times the repeat happens three or four years later. Repeat is at most monthly, but usually every five or six months." Another said, "I suppose this business is like others in that customers want the most expensive thing at the least price, but they only purchase products once or twice a year."

The process of making a sale also is quite an ordeal. While I was working in one unit, a customer came into the shop to order a sign.

"Hi. I own the restaurant down the street, and I'd like a small sign near our front door."

"OK." said the franchisee. "What do you want the sign to say?"

"Well, I want it to have our name, and the hours we're open. We're closed on Mondays."

"I see. What color do you want the sign to be?"

"I don't know. What do you think?"

"What are the colors in your restaurant? Sometimes people like to match those colors and sometimes they look for a color that compliments them."

"Well, what colors do you have?"

"All of them. We can do any color you want."

"I don't know what I want, that's why I asked you. You're the expert, aren't you?"

"Yes, but you have to give me something to go on. Do you want white letters? Where is the sign going to be, on the inside or the outside?"

"I don't know. Where do you think it should be?"

"What I mean is, is the sign going to be on a window, on your door, above the entrance, or somewhere else?

"I think the window would be good."

"OK, that sounds fine. If it's outside, over time it will become scratched. Kids touch it or pick at it, and it could also be affected by the weather."

"Well, if it has that many problems outside, why would you ask me if I wanted it outside?"

"Some people want the sign outside. We can do it either way. I need to know if it is going to be inside or outside so that it can be installed properly."

"OK, then, let's put it inside."

"Fine. Now what color would you like?"

He produced a color sheet and showed it to her. She looked carefully at the sheet and decided on a color.

"I think I want this red, here."

"OK, we'll go with that red. How big do you want the letters?"

"Oh, I don't know. Probably about this big." She gestured with her arms.

"Well, that's about fifteen inches. Now, what font do you want."

"What do you mean?"

"There are different fonts. It can be italicized, we can do block lettering, cursive, all sorts of different fonts."

"Well, let's just go with something simple."

"Now, see, that doesn't help me much because they're all simple."

"You know, this is really starting to aggravate me. You're asking me all sorts of questions about things I don't know. I only came in here to buy a sign, and you're making it into a big complicated process."

"Lady, I'm not making it complicated. I'm trying to help you design a sign that fits your business and looks the way you want it to look. How about this font? How does this look?"

"Fine. Whatever."

"Now, do you want the sign to be glossy, semi-glossy, or flat?"

She glared at him. "Do you have samples I could look at?"

"Yes." He brought out three types of vinyl and showed them to her.

"I'll go with the glossy. How much longer is this going to take? I didn't realize it would take this long. I'm on my lunch break and have to get back."

"We're almost done. Do you want us to install it?"

"Doesn't it come with installation?"

"No."

"Well, you'll have to. I don't know how to install it. Is it hard?"

"Not really, but if you make a mistake, if it is not lined up properly, then you would have to live with it. So you want us to install it?"

"Yes. Now, you'll be able to do it tomorrow, right?"

"Tomorrow?"

"Your sign says, you'll do it in twenty-four hours, guaranteed."

"The sign will be done tomorrow, but I won't be able to install it until the day after."

"So when you say, 'The right sign at the right price, guaranteed,' you really don't mean it."

"No. That's not right. You'll have your sign by tomorrow. I just can't install it tomorrow. If you want to install it, then it would be up tomorrow."

"Well, what are we talking for price here?"

"Just one last thing. Do you want a border?"

"A border? Around the sign?"

"Yes, a border."

"Well, I don't know. What do you think?"

"Let's not do the border. OK, let's see, The price will be sixty-two dollars."

"Now, I'm confused. Does that include installation or not?"

"No, with installation it will be ninety-seven dollars."

"So it will be ninety-seven dollars for the sign installed the day after tomorrow? OK."

The exchange between franchisee and restaurant owner lasted fifty-five minutes, and it was typical of the sales process in the business. A sign is truly a custom product, with a number of features that are unique and subject to personal taste, style, and aesthetics.

At a minimum, customers must decide what they want the sign to say and where it should be placed, as well as what color, letter size, and font they like. They must determine whether they will install it themselves. Both the customer and franchisee need to come to a common understanding because many of the options are interrelated, and a change in one aspect often forces a change in other aspects. For example, changing the font size slightly may make the sign too big to fit in the allotted space, it may mean that words have to be dropped or an extra line needs to be inserted. Of course, any variation in these factors could change the overall price. The task of selling a sign is not limited to educating customers about why a sign is necessary or how a particular sign can increase sales but also includes working with them to determine their tastes and preferences. It is never clear what particular style, message, or location will work best for a customer, and consequently there are no economies to scale. Franchisees must start anew with each customer.

The next day, the restaurant owner came back into the shop, and the franchisee brought out the completed sign.

"Oh. I can't use that," the restaurant owner declared.

"What! Why not? It's the sign you ordered!"

"I didn't realize it would be that big. It's too big. I don't think it will fit in the space."

"Yes, it will fit. I measured it, and it'll be no problem."

"But it looks too big to me, and the color doesn't seem right. It's too bright."

"Well, you chose that color. You must have known that the sign would be the color you chose."

"Well, obviously I didn't. I can't use the sign."

So that sign was scrapped. The specialized nature of sign making and the firm strategy embodied in the motto, "The right sign, at the right price, right away . . . guaranteed!" ensured that any mistake or unwanted sign would be absorbed by the franchisee.

Even larger customers can be difficult to manage. One franchisee described the pitfall of selling work to one such client. "I used to have a very good client, a museum downtown. They needed little signs on their display cases, exit signs, directions to other parts of the museum, you name it. They were probably doing about five thousand dollars per month in business alone. In this business, that's a really good customer. I got to know the guy, the purchase agent, and we hit it off pretty well. He would come in here, and we'd have a cup of coffee and talk about the business. He was really interested in the business. He wanted to know about different types of vinyl, the computer programs we used, and so on. I thought he was a nice guy and pretty bored with his job at the museum. Well, a couple months went by and I didn't hear from him and, you know, he was a regular customer, my best customer. So I called him up, and he said the museum didn't need my services anymore. He thought he could do it himself and convinced management that it would be cheaper to do it in-house. So I lost my best contract."

"But why sell them just little signs?"

"Well, that's the problem. There are technical constraints within the franchise system. We don't do electric signs, and we don't do neon, and these signs are more profitable. The biggest thing we can do is a banner. but even that has constraints. The other day I got a call to take down a banner on the twelfth floor of a building and replace it with a new one. I can do the banner fine, but we don't have the ability to take down and put up banners on the twelfth floor. So I didn't get the job."

Sign Masters franchisees are in a difficult position. While they often blame the ineptitude of Stu Beyer for their plight, the criticism is somewhat unfair since the nature of the sign industry also wreaks havoc. The specialized, idiosyncratic nature of the product means that franchisees have to spend an inordinate amount of time working with customers. It means there are few, if any, economies of scale. It means that most of the leads are all-or-nothing endeavors. Either a sign works or becomes a financial liability to be absorbed by the franchisee.

Because of increasing computer literacy and decreasing capital costs in computers, software, and CAD machines, competitors are increasing, margins are dropping, and the largest customers have the option of producing their own signs. The very technology that led to the birth of the industry can easily be adapted and learned by others and that makes the "make or buy" decision a simple calculation. Stu Beyer certainly contributed to the financial woes of many franchisees by designing a franchise system with a limited range of services, and he perpetuated their troubles with a poor marketing strategy, poor technical and franchisee support, and weak criteria for franchisee selection.

But the main culprit is the inappropriate use of franchising to this particular industry. Custom products and franchising are strange bedfellows.

# CHAPTER 5

STAR MUFFLER

"What did you do before buying your franchise?" I asked Walter, who was a large, barrel-chested man about fifty years old.

"I delivered milk. I was a milk truck driver," he replied.

"Really? We have our milk delivered."

He stared at me in disbelief. "You're shitting me."

"No, I'm serious. There are a lot of people in my neighborhood that do."

Walter let out a long sigh and slouched back into his chair

"Fuck!" he boomed out, as his face turned bright red. "I can't fucking believe it!"

He leaned forward in his chair and put his hand across his brow. "That was the best job I ever had. I mean, you wake up early, you're out in the country, driving a truck. No one looking over your shoulder telling you what to do. But by the mid-80s, the market was gone. I mean, completely gone. I had to quit because there wasn't enough business to support my family."

He looked at me again with a puzzled look. "Really, there are *a lot* of people who get their milk delivered now?"

"Yeah, I think so, at least on our street."

"Who is it? Who does it?"

"I don't know. Some guy in his 30s—"

"No, I mean, which company?"

"Oh, I don't know their name, but we get it delivered once a week."

"Hmmm." He pondered for a moment. "I wonder if I could get back into it?"

"I don't know, I think the market must be better now because there seem to be pretty many people who get their milk delivered."

While we were talking in his back office, a commotion erupted in the customer waiting room. Walter got up and headed in that direction, where he found a well-dressed elderly gentleman speaking with Ray, the front desk manager.

"I was just here this morning," the gentleman stated.

"I know," said Ray, "I remember you. But this is not our doing."

The man had his brakes worked on earlier in the day and then returned, which Walter instantly took as an ominous sign. He listened to the customer's complaint, growing increasingly irritated until he could contain himself no longer. His face turned bright red and the veins on his neck popped out.

"I'm telling ya," Walter said in a raised voice to the older man, "those aren't my parts!"

"Then whose parts are they? I took the car to the car dealership after I left here, and they said you put the brakes on wrong. Do you know how I found out? I was driving down the expressway and my brakes went out, that's how."

"Look, I'll be right back," Walter said as he stormed out of the office into the back room. He returned with his arms full of parts. "See here?" he yelled. "These are your parts." He dumped an armload of parts onto the counter.

The customer looked quizzically at Walter. "I don't understand what those parts have to do with the parts you put on."

"Now, look at these parts carefully. See 'em? These parts that you brought in are different than the ones I put on. How can I be responsible for parts falling off if they're different than the ones here?"

"Well, all I know is that I've never had my brakes go out on me before. I came in here to get the brakes worked on and within fifteen minutes of leaving here, they malfunctioned. It seems pretty clear to me that there is an association between coming here and malfunctioning brakes."

"No! That's what I'm saying. It looks like a coincidence, but we had nothing to do with it! We never even touched these bad parts!"

"Well, I want to know what you're going to do to correct the situation."

"I'm not going to do a goddamn thing because they're NOT MY PARTS!" shouted Walter.

"Who are you? Are you the manager?"

"No, I'm the owner. This is my shop, and you're not getting anything from me. It's not my fault."

"Well, then, whose fault is it? Are you telling me it's my fault that the brakes went out fifteen minutes after leaving here?"

"That's what I'm telling you. The parts that broke down had nothing to do with us."

"Fine. Let's fix it under the warranty."

"It's not covered under the warranty. I won't do it under the warranty because those aren't my parts!"

Now the customer became visibly angry. "So you're telling me that you're not going to honor a warranty that's two hours old?"

"Yeah. That's what I'm telling you."

The customer gathered up the parts on the table. "What is the number for the corporate office? This is despicable."

"It's right there on your receipt, the 800 number," stated Walter.

The customer left, and Walter returned to his office just outside of the customer waiting room. "Sorry about that. It's just that with this economy I'm short-tempered. I've only given money back to one customer in the last five years. If I'm wrong, sure, no problem. But when I know I'm right, then the customer is wrong and I ain't giving any money back."

"Does that happen very often here?"

"That? No, not that often. He'll probably call Corporate, but I don't care."

"How do you know he isn't a CEO or something?"

"Well, he was driving a Ford Fairmont, for Christ's sake."

Walter laughed. "I don't think he's a CEO." Walter leaned back in his chair toward the customer waiting room. "Hey, Ray," he yelled, "maybe we should be scared. That guy was probably a big CEO, or maybe he was sent here by Corporate to test us." They both had a good laugh at the prospect.

"I'm just not in a good mood. About everything that could go wrong, has. It's been one thing after another, and it seems to be getting worse. The very first day I was left on my own to operate the store, and I didn't have the expertise—that's why I bought a franchise in the first place. Oh, I knew something about cars—I love cars—but I didn't know anything about this business," Walter explained. "I thought by buying a franchise I'd get help on things but the first day—nothing. They got a 'turnkey' operation here. They turn the key and walk away. No, I'm serious. I had to learn the fucking business from a competitor down the street, a Midas guy of all things. I'd call up the guy and ask him, 'What do I do about this? How do you handle this situation?'—you know, stuff like that."

"He told you what to do?" I asked.

"Hell, yeah. He didn't care. It sounds crazy, but that's what happened."

"But what are your problems now? You've been operating for five years, and I see customers in the waiting room. How are things now?"

"Now? Shit. I got labor problems like you can't believe. There's no loyalty here. Absolutely none. I don't have one guy working that was here two years ago. It's just a constant cycle of turnover. The dealerships don't have a problem with turnover, but I can't pay $16.00 per hour like those guys."

"Well, why do they leave?"

"Money, and they'll make threats. If you come down hard on 'em they'll say, 'I'm going to go to the dealership.' You know, they play you against the other guy. But that's not the main thing when I say I got labor problems. The main thing is I can't trust anyone to watch the shop while I'm gone. That's why I got my son working with me. One of us has to be here all the time. I'll give you an example. A month ago my niece had her wedding on a Saturday. Well, I didn't get to go—I didn't get to go to my own niece's wedding! I had to stay here to watch the shop. Somebody has to be here all the time because of the trust factor. See that shop right over there?"

He pointed across the parking lot and street. "A guy brought a Corvette in, and the shop told him it would have to stay overnight, and they took the damn car down to Rush Street. They just took the guy's car. That's the mentality of the guys working in this business—not the owners, I mean the installers. That's their mentality. What the fuck do they care if they take a guy's car downtown?"

"Is that what you mean by trust? You can't trust them to keep away from customers' cars?"

"No, not just that. That's their mentality. But they're a bunch of cheats. Employees take jobs from the company, from me. A customer will come in and complain a little bit about the price or something. They'll want to talk to the installer to see if they really need the work done, and the installer will say something like, 'Look, buddy, I can't do anything for you on the price. But if you bring it over to my house on Sunday, I can take care of it for you for, you know, a helluva lot less.' Now, see, that causes a lot of problems for me. Is that work covered under the warranty? No way. I won't honor anything that's done outside of the shop, but the customer will say, 'Your own guy did it!' I mean, Christ! You know what the assholes at Corporate will say? They'll say, 'The customer is always right.' Well, fuck that. It's my business, and I'll decide if I'm giving money back."

## THE STAR MUFFLER WAY

Walter's combative and belligerent approach to customers was not endorsed by Star Muffler but, quite the opposite, was completely at odds with the corporate philosophy. Walter epitomized the monumental task facing Mark Spinelli, Star Muffler's chief executive officer, of transforming "car guys" into managers. As Walter's experience indicated, it was often a difficult, if not impossible, transition for franchisees to make. For Spinelli, it was a battle he had been waging for the better part of two decades.

"How much do you know about the undercar industry?" Spinelli asked me during our first meeting.

"Not much," I replied.

"Well, let me give you a quick history. During the 1970s, auto services franchises popped up overnight," explained Spinelli, "both because of increased demand and also because entrepreneurs found that they could make a lot of money through franchising. Star Muffler started in 1975 with this idea in mind, but there was no strong concept by the owner. The owner recruited people who knew little about the automobile repair business, took their money, and then blamed them for failing. After losing money for five years, the franchisees revolted, and Star Muffler was sold in 1980 to a tail and muffler firm.

"But things weren't much better with the new company. They really just used Star as a distribution system to move its product. They had an accounting focus, and their only goal was to add more units, create more royalties, and push product. We were always the 'stepchild' of the company, and since they had a hands-off management policy, we lost $500,000 to $800,000 per year. Finally, in 1988 we said to the parent company, 'Hey, you know this is not the way to run the business. Let us buy it from you and run it the way it should be run.' They agreed, so we bought the company."

"What did you get when you bought the company?" I asked.

"We knew what we were getting into since we had all been with the company when it was owned by the tail and muffler company, but we only had potential, we didn't have a strong concept, we didn't have a strong trademark, and a lot of the guys were not qualified to be franchisees."

"So what did you do?"

"After we bought the company, we looked around to see which franchisees were successful and which were not. Although we wanted to grow the company, you can't take the blind, stick them in a store, and then take their money. So we wanted to have a development approach where we could train franchisees to operate according to our procedures, and if they don't want to, then we weed them out.

"We looked at our highest volume franchisee, Pete Morgan, and noticed that his volume had nothing to do with location. In fact, he's located in a poor, mostly minority neighborhood and he has a lot of competition nearby. But he does have a unique approach in dealing with his employees and customers. He trains his workers well, pays them well, but he holds them accountable and responsible for things in the store. We took his approach and 'Morganized' it—we broadened it and now teach it to all of our franchisees."

"So what does that mean, really?"

"It means that we're in the business of developing employees, and as a footnote to that, we're in the car service business," Spinelli explained.

Star Muffler now has annual revenues of thirty million dollars, fifty-two franchisees in five states, and a cohesive strategy in the undercar industry. Star has two main product lines: exhaust systems and brakes. The demand for exhaust systems dropped significantly in the early 1990s compared with previous years, and there is a threat that auto manufacturers, who already have the technology, may make exhaust systems that never wear out. If battery-operated vehicles become widespread, then the exhaust side of Star's business would suffer significantly. But brakes, which comprised 50–60 percent of Star's revenues, should continue to be a profitable segment of the market.

Even so, Star faces several obstacles within the industry: a lack of differentiation among service providers and a poor industry image. The lack of differentiation means that any muffler and brake firm is a perfect, or at least adequate, substitute for the services of Star Muffler. Competition therefore revolves around price. For example, a franchisee will charge $9.99 for an oil change, which is below cost, just for the opportunity to offer the customer additional services. Spinelli attempted to make Star a niche player in a market with few niches. The cornerstone of his approach involved treating customers as long-term partners rather than preying upon them as easy targets. But customer experience, like that of the older gentleman at Walter's shop described above, was often negative.

"Every sale is a negative one because the customer doesn't want to be there and only comes in when there's a problem," said Spinelli.

"I know," I replied. "I happened to be in one of your shops when a customer came back to report a problem, and the franchisee became enraged."

"Who was that? Can you tell me?"

"No, I can't."

Spinelli thought for a moment. "It must have been Walter. See, we think Walter spends too much time in the shop. He's over-involved, he's too close to all the details of the operations, and we're trying to get him out of there."

"You mean you're trying to terminate him?"

"No, I mean we're trying to find him a second shop. He's a good guy, and we want him in our system, but he doesn't do well as a single-shop owner. We think by getting a second shop he won't be able to be quite so domineering to employees and customers."

"But, the negative image, is that particular to Star Muffler or—"

"No," Spinelli replied, "that's a problem with the industry. Look, everybody knows that the poor worker, the guy who can't read, goes to the local service station for a job. The image of the installer is that he's a drug addict, divorced, or has a criminal record, so consumers don't trust him. And we understand that. We're trying to address that at the moment."

"How are you doing that?"

"In several ways. We think the negative image of the industry is partly because of installers, but it is also because of franchisees. For installers, we designed a college tuition program modeled after the U.S. Armed Forces system that pays workers to go to college for each year they worked at a franchise system. Most of our good employees are guys who wouldn't normally go to college four years straight but would work their way through, maybe go to a community college for a time and then transfer to a four-year school.

"The type of employee that is a manager at a shop is someone who would be a manager at a Bennigan's [a restaurant chain], and we designed it with this person in mind. We're basically looking for employees that will be more responsible and motivated because we know that those employees will serve franchisees, and ultimately customers, well. For franchisees we're recruiting people from outside the industry because we don't want the bad habits of the industry."

But current franchisees disagree with that strategy. One franchisee with experience in a dealership service center voiced a common concern: "They let guys in now without any car knowledge whatsoever. You need a vocabulary, a knowledge to talk to people. If you don't know what you're talking about, you can't tell people what to do."

But, according to Spinelli, it is the operations of the system that are important, and new franchisees can be taught to understand and implement the new system. "We're on the cutting edge on operations," said Spinelli. "Our products aren't different from any other muffler firm, but we don't make money on product, we make money on the royalty. The successful franchise system needs to allow franchisees to control the cost of goods. Either the franchisee has to be able to get alternate sources of supply or he has to have the ability to change prices to take advantage of consumer tastes and local competition."

The biggest hurdle for Spinelli has been eradicating the old attitude, which exploits customer ignorance. "I can find anything wrong with anyone's car," stated one of the more successful franchisees in the system. Another responded, "In the business we're in, you've got to repair as many things right now as you can because people are more transient, less loyal. Suppose a guy comes into the shop with a loud muffler and we take a look at it, you know, put it on the lift, and tell him that he needs a new muffler and tail pipe—about a sixty buck job. When we're done, we fire it up and there's a loud noise. So we look closer and find a hole on top of the exhaust pipe—somewhere that we couldn't see before. Who's right? I mean, a deal's a deal so we tell the guy, you know, 'Sir, I'm sorry I made a mistake on your car, but we'll fix it up, no charge.' So, that's the way it goes, but we'll get him next time."

The idea that franchisees will "get" the customer next time indicates just how difficult it will be for Spinelli to integrate the new customer-concerned approach into the existing company. Part of the difficulty stems from Star Muffler itself: what the company views as taking care of the customer, the franchisee sees as "selling up." For instance, one franchisee told me that Corporate was always telling him to increase his volume of shock absorbers. "They keep telling me, 'Your shock sales are down! Your shock sales are down!' But how do they know what my shock sales should be? They use these national statistics that give them some percentage of cars that need shocks, but there's no substitute for looking at the car. I don't know, maybe the roads are smoother out here by me, but I'm not like Sears. I won't sell at the expense of honesty." Another franchisee responded, "It's real easy to sit back and tell us that shock sales are down, but it's another thing to look a customer in the face and tell him that he needs new shocks. You know, the customer will say, 'Show me why I need new shocks,' so you go out and push on the car and it doesn't bounce up and down and there's no leak. It's a lot harder to tell a customer that they need shocks when they really don't."

I once mentioned the shock sales to Spinelli. He rolled his eyes. "I know there are some guys out there that disagree with us on this, but we know what the shock sales should be because we use pretty sophisticated marketing techniques. But the reason shock sales are down is not because the roads are smoother, but because the franchisee forgets to make the sale. The franchisee is not following the operating procedure that we have. In large measure, the operating system involves franchisees asking customers about various potential problems in their car. But these guys don't do that."

The new customer-friendly strategy of Star Muffler was not highly regarded by current franchisees. As one stated, "What they're trying to do is to develop the old-fashioned neighborhood service station, but the customer's loyalty is to the guy they trust, not to the name Star Muffler." And another remarked, "They want to do image advertising, but incentive advertising is what brings customers in. The majority of my customers buy because of me. The only people that use coupons are my repeat customers—people that would come in anyway."

To improve the image and consistency of the shops, Spinelli introduced a new program to rate shops on cleanliness and other factors. Spinelli hoped that the image questionnaire would be more objective since franchisees would know what they were being rated on. The program looked effective on paper, but it caused dissension among franchisees. During an advisory board meeting between several franchisees, Spinelli, and other corporate officers, the difficulty in instituting the program became clear.

"This maintenance and image questionnaire is unfair," said Rocky, a franchisee.

"How so?" responded the corporate field man in charge of rating the shops.

"Look, I have my windows cleaned on Wednesday, and on Thursday morning a lady with two kids comes in and the kids spend their time with their faces against the window, putting smudge marks on it, putting their grimy hands on it. And I get knocked off for that."

"Well, that's the way it goes."

"But the windows were clean for Christ's sake the day before. It's unfair for me to get knocked down for that. I mean, suppose my guys are humping—I'm not gonna pull a guy off of a job so he can clean windows. That's bullshit!"

"But that's what the customer sees when he walks in, so that's the way it has to be. Besides, maybe the next time the windows will be clean but the bathroom won't be."

"I don't care, I think it's bullshit that we get knocked down."

"Yeah," the field man said as he looked over the questionnaire, "but windows are only four out of one hundred points."

"So what. You could still lose by one point."

"Well, what's your idea? Do you have a better way to measure the image the customer sees going in to the shop?"

"No," said Rocky, "I don't have a better way. That's your job. I just think you're putting too much weight on something like windows, and I'm not going to pull a guy off a job to clean some goddamn windows."

"I understand that. No one's asking you to pull guys off to clean windows. That's not the point. The point is to make you aware of what the customer sees when they walk into the shop."

"OK," Mark Spinelli broke in, "I think it's important to have the maintenance and image questionnaire, so why don't we take the average of the scores? Or, maybe we take the top three out of six scores. Would that work better?"

"That's better," replied Rocky. "I don't disagree with the image questionnaire, I just think you have to understand where I'm coming from."

"What's a good award for the top shop?" asked Spinelli. "Dinner?"

"I don't know," said another franchisee, "where do you want to go, Pete?" This referred to Pete Morgan, the top revenue-producing franchisee.

"This isn't rigged!" said the field man. "What makes you think that Pete is going to win?"

"He wins everything else."

"Well, you're questioning my integrity. You're saying that I'm not fair in my judgments. Is that what you're saying?"

The franchisee looked down at his papers and ignored the question. After an awkward silence, Spinelli broke in again. "So is dinner a good award for the top franchisee?"

"No," said Rocky. "The award should go to the shop guys since they're the ones to do the work."

"Dinner?" Spinelli asked again.

"No, they don't want dinner."

"How about shoes—comfortable walking shoes with steel toes," offered Walter.

"Yeah. Christ, I tell ya," said Rocky, "these guys will not buy shoes. I came in the other day and a guy is wearing tennis shoes and I say to him, 'Do you know what would happen if you dropped something on your foot?' and he says to me, 'I ain't gonna drop nothin.' I mean, shit! You just can't get them to wear the shoes!"

"I pay half," said Walter, "but the more you give them, the more they take."

"Do they wear the shoes?" asked Spinelli.

"No, not all the time."

The advisory board meeting concluded and the franchisees agreed that the maintenance and image questionnaire results would be averaged and that only the top three out of six scores would be used to rate shops. But the passion surrounding the mere change from a subjective rating system to a more objective one highlights the management problems Spinelli faced. In keeping with his customer-oriented business model, Spinelli merely wanted to ensure that franchisee shops would be clean so that customers would have a pleasant experience. But franchisees did not view it that way. They viewed a clean shop as a task that would hurt profits.

The maintenance and image questionnaire, while relatively benign in terms of impact, highlights just how difficult it is for franchisors to institute changes within the system. A more nettlesome problem for Spinelli, and the linchpin of his drive toward a customer-friendly Star Muffler, was a systemwide warranty.

FREE RIDERS

The profitability of each franchise unit and the relationship between franchisees have been altered by Spinelli's new customer-oriented strategy. In the old business model, franchisees routinely treated customers much the way Walter did the older gentleman. Of course, the old attitudes fostered customer distrust and disloyalty and discouraged repeat business. To overcome this distrust, Spinelli instituted a systemwide warranty on parts and labor. While the warranty added consistency to the whole chain, individual franchisees absorbed the cost of the warranty work. Naturally, franchisees kept close tabs on the original shop for which they made repairs, and conflicts over warranty work led to bitter rivalries throughout the system. During a lull in a franchisee meeting, one such conflict erupted.

"Hey, Dougie!" called out one franchisee. "Do all your installers have their head up their ass or are you doing the work yourself?"

"Fuck you."

"No, really. How 'bout I send over one of my guys to teach your guys how to put a couple of hangers on right. It'd be a helluva lot cheaper for me."

"Hey, fuck you. If I had a nickel for each one of your shitty jobs that comes through my shop, I could've retired five years ago."

"Yeah? Well, I spent a thousand bucks on your crap last week alone."

Mark Spinelli interrupted before things got out of hand. "Guys, you have to keep this in perspective. The reason we have the warranty is, first, because it is the right thing to do. And second, we need to help the customer get over the negative image in our industry. Our numbers are up across the system, and our satisfaction rating is higher than any other muffler and brake shop. And the reason why is because of our approach to customers. The warranty is a big part of that, and we need to honor the warranty, regardless of who did the original work."

While franchisees understood the importance and necessity of a system-wide warranty, they didn't like it, especially if they absorbed a lot of warranties in a short time period. It was common for new franchisees to absorb more warranty claims than experienced franchisees. As one said, "When I first took over the store, I was bombarded with warranty work. I mean, these people were coming out of the woodwork with problems. If it's a problem with product, you've got to bite the bullet, but if it is a problem of workmanship then it should be the responsibility of the franchisee." Another franchisee commented, "We need a warranty, but I only cover it if it's a problem with the part. If the problem is because of some installer for another franchisee, then I don't cover it because that doesn't solve the problem."

"Well," I asked, "it's a systemwide warranty. How can you get out of that?"

"Oh, you can get out of it easy enough. Look, I have to absorb the warranty. The customer don't want to go back to the original store because he figures that place messed it up, so he goes to a different store. You could get unlucky and absorb a lot, especially if the guys around you aren't doing a good job. But a lot of franchisees, when a warranty comes in, will tell the customer, 'Sorry, but I don't have that part in stock.' So they just don't do warranty work."

The systemwide warranty is a step in the right direction as far as consistency and standards go, but Star Muffler still had a long way to go. Mark Spinelli once confided to me, "We had a suitor who wanted to buy a major stake in a number of franchise units several years ago, but declined because the stores were so inconsistent that he felt the operation was not a franchise system. He could see no system in use." And no wonder. Throughout the system, there are stores with different layouts, different color schemes, and different sign placements, tag lines, and fonts. Although Spinelli hoped to change the colors, franchisees resisted any changes that involved out-of-pocket expenses. In most cases, Spinelli had few choices other than franchisee goodwill. One franchisee told me, "Spinelli told me that I couldn't buy a new shop until the new colors were put on my old shop. I'm interested in change for improvement, but not for change's sake. I mean, look at McDonald's. They got the golden arches, and they've always had the golden arches. You don't see those guys changing colors for the hell of it. We need to decide on a color scheme and stick with it, not change every couple of years just because we need to spruce up the place."

Overall, the warranty system, the image and maintenance program, and the focus on customer satisfaction has made some impact in changing the old practices of Star Muffler, and the increased market share and customer loyalty can be attributed to them. But one program that did not seem to work so well was the college tuition program. It was designed to provide franchisees with a reliable source of labor but ignored the critical uncertainty that franchisees face with employees, which is not so much turnover, but trust.

I once asked Mark Spinelli, "Why do you think most of these guys bought a Star Muffler franchise?"

"Probably because they don't have to work on Sundays, and it's hard for the employees to walk off with the inventory," he responded.

But franchisees were vulnerable to their employees in a number of ways beyond mere inventory. As one franchisee said, "You got to watch the employees write the tickets." Another franchisee told me that he has had only two vacations in eight and a half years. "Last month, I got back and my employees had stolen seven hundred dollars in cash. How do you like that? I'm almost trapped here."

# CHAPTER 6

SOCIAL PROFILE OF FRANCHISEES

I pulled into the parking lot at a Chicago convention center early one Saturday morning. Streams of people were moving toward the entrance, where a crowd had been gathering waiting for the opening of the franchise expo. Franchise expos are held once a year in the largest metropolitan areas and draw hundreds or thousands of people from across the region. The crowd waiting for the start of the Chicago franchise expo appeared to be a fairly representative cross-section of Americans, representative, that is, based on ascriptive characteristics: African American, Hispanic, white, males and females, neither young nor old but decidedly middle-aged. At the franchise expo, franchisors market their franchise system, products, and services to potential franchisees. It was the anticipation of being the first person to acquire a particular franchise that fueled the crowd, and there was a certain excitement and exuberance among those present.

Inside, franchisors had set up booths with brochures and videos about their concepts, and they staffed them with several sales representatives or even the founders themselves, if it was a new franchise concept, in order to promote the business. It was here that potential franchisees gathered firsthand ideas on the latest franchise concepts, talked to the franchisor, assessed the opportunities, and purchased a franchise. The franchise expo is the premier marketplace where much of the interaction between franchisors and potential franchisees occurs, and it can be very profitable for franchisors. One salesman estimated that his company had "sold three franchises directly from two franchise expo shows last year. The investment level for our franchisees is about $170,000 each. Our investment in each show is about $3,000." Another franchisor said, "We're a new franchise and have only done one franchise expo show so far. The first time out we got 419 personal applications. It will take us another three to four weeks to follow up on all of them. Six people signed the disclosure documents right there at the booth. It's now several days after the show, and the phone has been ringing off the hook—prospects are frantically pleading with us to reserve their territory. Most said that our booth was so jammed they couldn't get to see us."

Since the franchise expo could lead to hundreds of prospects and potential sales of several hundred thousand dollars, it came as no surprise that there was a wide variety of franchise concepts from which to choose: hair salons, automobile glass, automobile oil change, concrete work, recycling (scrap metal), commercial and residential cleaning, dry cleaning, printing shops, restaurants, lawn care, advertising, tax preparation. Notably absent, however, were some of the most established franchise systems such as McDonald's, Burger King, Wendy's, Blockbuster, JiffyLube, and nearly all of the hotel chains. What's left then? Nothing other than the greatest assortment of entrepreneurial ideas in the United States—some doomed to failure, but others on their way to becoming wildly successful.

It was this expectation, this hope of riches, that drove people to the franchise expo in the first place. Though early in the morning, the convention center was crowded with aspiring entrepreneurs, some literally dashing quickly from one exhibit to the next. Multitudes of people gathered at particular franchise systems that were supposedly "hot." Today, it seemed that the hot businesses were those that provided sign graphics, like Sign Masters, and there were long queues to receive literature on some of these franchise systems. There was also a pizza franchise that was doing quite well, and it garnered considerable interest later in the day when it gave out free pizza slices. "It's a marketing tool for us," a sales manager told me. "We think the pizza is really good, and we're more than happy to have potential franchisees try it out. After all, it's the pizza that we're selling."

"Does having free pizza ever lead to anything, besides content prospects?" I asked.

"Oh yeah. It's great. We've gotten several potential franchisees just because they like the pizza," he replied.

In other franchise systems, it was not quite so clear what was being sold. One franchisor was apparently selling phone services, and he had a complex graphic display of the concept. As I began to sort through the information, a very attractive, scantily clad blond woman approached me. "You look like you're pretty interested in our franchise."

"Well, I'm just trying to figure out what's going on here."

"I tell you what, we're inviting interested people downstairs to a smaller room to give them a better sense of the opportunities."

"But I can't even figure out what the franchise is."

"We basically sell reduced phone rates to corporate clients, but I think you'll find the presentation downstairs will answer your questions."

"I see. Well, I would normally be interested, but I'm a researcher from the University of Chicago and don't think I fit your profile."

She didn't understand me or didn't care.

"You're not interested at all? This is a great opportunity. It'll only take fifteen minutes."

"Fifteen minutes? Well, I guess so."

So I was led downstairs by Robert, the other sales representative, to a small conference room. Inside were three men in suits and an easel with a chart depicting what I assumed to be growth, since the only item on the chart was a line from the lower left corner skyrocketing toward the upper right corner. I soon realized that the line was the expected profits one could earn from the franchise. I was the only prospect there. After introductions, the lead sales representative said, "OK, then, why don't we start?"

"Will there be anyone else joining or am I the only one?"

"It's to your advantage to be the only one. This is such a terrific opportunity by the end of the day we won't have any territories left. You're in the position to grab the prime locations."

"OK, but I'm just here for information."

"Fine. I understand that, and that's a smart thing to do. But here's another smart thing: listen to what we have to say and then get your checkbook ready because you're not going to want to miss this opportunity and, like I said, by the end of the day there won't be anything left. Now, you're tired of working for other people, right?"

"Um, I guess so."

"Of course you are! And how much money do you make in your job?"

"I don't have a job right now, I'm in school."

"OK, fine, but if you did have a job what do you think you'd be making? Or, let me put it this way, what will you be making when you graduate?"

"I don't know, probably around forty-five thousand."

"That's pretty good, but with this opportunity, you can easily triple that. Easily. Now, how would you like that?"

"Pretty good."

"You bet! Now here's the best part: you don't even have to work hard to do it. Our system is so simple that it generates income—on a monthly basis—and you don't have to do anything."

"Well, what is your system?"

"Hey," he laughed along with the other two guys, "that's just it. What if I tell you all the secrets of this opportunity, how we make money, what our expansion plans are, the tricks of the trade? How do I know who you are? You could be a competitor. I can't tell you everything unless you're willing to sign on. Otherwise, you could walk out of here and compete with us, and we'd be pretty dumb salesmen to give away our trade secrets for nothing. How much can you write a check for right now?"

"Right now? I don't even know what you're selling!"

"OK. This is the deal. In urban markets across the country, we sign up corporate clients to run their phone service through us. Nothing changes in how they are billed, nothing changes in their rates, but since we have all these accounts we can strike a better deal with the phone companies. In effect, we become their biggest customer."

"But couldn't the companies just work out a deal with AT&T or whomever?"

"They could, but they don't. They don't want to negotiate with AT&T over a few cents! That means absolutely nothing to them. It would be a waste of their time to even contemplate something like that! This is the perfect opportunity. In a large metropolitan area, there are thousands of companies and each one of those is a potential client. In some cases we already have corporate clients set up so you can hit the ground running. Now, I've told you more than I should because you could walk out of here armed with that information and become my competitor. What's it going to take to get you to sign on right now? What do I have to do to convince you that this is the opportunity of a lifetime?"

"I just have one question. Why do you need franchisees at all? If this is such a good opportunity, why don't you do this yourself?"

"Fair enough. We can't penetrate the market quick enough. We want to be a national presence in this market within six months, and the only way we can do that is by franchising. Now how much can you write a check for right now to secure your area?"

"I can't write a check for anything."

"Nothing? Are you crazy? Are you going to pass up a six-figure income for forty-five thousand? Really! What could be better than this? Do you want to work in a restaurant and deal with teenage employees? Do you want to work in some janitorial business and have to manage people that don't even speak English? You can do this from your own home! There is absolutely no overhead, and once companies sign on they never change the contract. Why would they? Look, I'm telling you, do yourself a favor and take advantage of this opportunity. Quit trying to make life so hard. We'll sell every single territory by three this afternoon. You're the first one here, and you have your choice of any location in the nation."

"I'm sorry. It sounds like a really good opportunity . . . "

"It is."

"But I'm just not at a point in my life where I can take advantage of it. Thanks for the information."

"OK, if that's the way it's going to be, then that's the way it is. Good luck."

I could not get out of the room fast enough. When I emerged on the main floor of the franchise expo, I understood quite clearly that franchisors and franchisees share one very important value: the belief in the American Dream of entrepreneurship and all that it encompasses—independence, freedom, and wealth. Many franchisors at the expo were living that dream. The small, start-up franchise system was often the brainchild of a lone entrepreneur, and by franchising the concept he or she had the opportunity to build an empire, like Ray Kroc of McDonald's.

Franchisees were prepared to buy that dream, and it was often merely an issue of selecting which opportunity one would buy. The American Dream is a powerful motivator, and its effects were felt throughout the franchise expo as franchisors attempted to lure franchisees into their fold. The expo was not only a place to learn about the latest business ideas from some of the leading entrepreneurs, but it also offered insight into the engine behind franchise systems: franchisees.

Who were these people? What were their motivations? What types of careers had they had, and what were they hoping to achieve in franchising? Some of them would make the most important and consequential decision of their lives at the convention center by purchasing a franchise. Who would do that?

I learned something more about franchisees, or potential franchisees, the following week when I attended a special seminar hosted by a franchisor in the maintenance and janitorial business. The seminar was billed as an "informational meeting" to learn more about the maintenance industry and was held in a conference room in a local hotel. The company that hosted the event was a competitor of King Cleaners and consequently faced the same obstacles in the market and shared many of the same characteristics as King Cleaners. The costs to enter were relatively low (under $20,000), there were few skills required of the franchisee, all territories were available, and the market was billed as "recession-resistant" because, as the company flyer stated, "Everything gets dirty, we're not a fad!" The seminar was attended by fewer than ten people, myself included, and was hosted by two vice presidents from the company. Both men were in their late 50s or early 60s, well-dressed, but rather ordinary in their presentation style.

During the morning session, the leaders focused on financing the business opportunity, and there were even a few direct questions to the attendees about how they would scrape up enough money to purchase a territory. It was during one of these question and answer exchanges that it came to light that five of the participants were all related. An African American family consisting of a brother and his wife, two sisters, and one nephew were pooling their money (and labor) to buy a franchise and start their own business. This development was very intriguing to the franchise vice presidents, and the African Americans vaulted from speculators to solid prospects. The seminar took a turn from an informative fact-gathering meeting to a fairly high-fevered sales pitch for the franchise.

We later retired to a room down the hall to a catered lunch, and the meeting became much more social. Both vice presidents made the rounds talking with the prospective franchisees. Of course, nothing really changed other than our move across the hall to the dining area, but the vice presidents—seasoned sales managers—took the opportunity to find out more about the participants, why they were there, what their careers had been, and what attracted them to the company. All of this information would be woven into the second half of the presentation, after lunch. One middle-aged woman was divorced and had a settlement payment that could be used to finance the business.

Another couple had a small inheritance that they would use, and of course, the African Americans had their pooled resources. That left me as the lone wild card, the puzzle to be figured out.

"You seem pretty busy taking notes," one executive said to me. It was not too difficult to figure that out since I had spent the morning taking copious notes of the proceedings. "You must be interested in franchising."

"Yes," I replied. "I have some interest in franchising, but I'm not sure where it will lead."

"What do you think about our opportunity? Have you thought about building maintenance?"

"Well, I'm really undecided, and I'm just starting my investigation of possibilities. I don't think I'll be making any significant decisions today."

"I see," he responded. "You're more than welcome to stay for the afternoon, but I have to tell you that we'll be speaking more directly to the people who are serious about our opportunity today."

"What sorts of things will you cover?" I asked.

"We will cover our business system, the reporting arrangements, the accounting procedures we use. How to keep track of inventory. Hiring procedures that franchisees may want to consider, and marketing."

"I see. Maybe I'll bow out of that part of the seminar then."

"Listen, why don't you stay for lunch? It's free, and we have way more than we could possibly eat."

So I took him up on the offer and stayed through lunch. It was a fairly productive and informative lunch for me because I learned something about prospective franchisees and the sales process companies use to solicit them. An "informational seminar" was an ideal way to bring in prospective franchisees, in part because it appeared to be neutral since it was just "informational." The seminar also provided an opportunity for the franchisor to rule out inappropriate franchisees such as myself. People who lacked an interest in the franchise would be encouraged to leave midway through the seminar. Then, with a select group of potential serious franchisees, the real sales process could proceed. If successful, the franchisor could sell three franchises and net over $60,000 for the day.

As I left the seminar, I began to feel that the profile of franchisees I was formulating was somehow related to the maintenance industry itself. Franchises in the maintenance industry are some of the most affordable units available, and with relatively unsophisticated products and services, perhaps these opportunities appealed to a unique group of potential buyers. I needed to determine whether the profile I was finding was specific to the maintenance industry or whether it was a profile that would be found throughout franchising.

It seemed that my methodology was partly to blame: How reliable were seminars or expos for developing a profile of franchisees? Not very. Although the maintenance industry seminar was insightful in terms of how some franchisees became familiar with a particular system, I doubt that I could generalize these findings to anything substantial. So I determined to alter my methodology and began to develop a profile of franchisees by working alongside them rather than attending conventions and shows with them.

The profile that emerged was based upon this close association and, not too surprisingly, differed significantly from the received notions of industry insiders—the consultants, advisors, attorneys, and other business people who populate the franchise domain. According to industry insiders, there was a profile of franchisees that already existed, and the task for the savvy franchisor was to separate out the potentially bad franchisees from the good ones. One influential franchise consultant at a seminar intended for entrepreneurs debating whether or not to franchise their business made the following remarks:

"There's a certain profile of franchisee that you want to recruit because we know that these people do really well in franchise systems, they thrive while others fail. I have to tell you, an entrepreneur makes the worst franchisee. You might think that they would do well, but it is just the opposite. For one thing, they'll never listen to you. Also, they won't follow the system, and they'll cause problems in your system for the entire contract, and believe me, twenty years— the typical length of a contract—is a long time to put up with someone like that. You don't want any creative thinkers, either. Again, these people will not follow your system, and instead they'll look for ways to do their own thing.

"You want someone who follows the rules. It's said that the 'A' student works for the 'B' manager who works for the 'C' owner or entrepreneur. You want the 'A' students, and you should look at their grades. They might give you funny looks after all these years, but I'm serious here, grades are a good indication of how someone will do in franchising. Also, look to see if they have any speeding tickets—people that follow the rules will not have any."

The consultant looked around the room at the forty or so people and asked, "Everybody who has at least one speeding ticket in the last six months raise your hand."

Almost all of the hands went up amid laughter.

"See, you guys are the entrepreneurs. There are not enough hours in the day for you, you're always juggling several things, always running late, always trying to do too many things at once. Do not hire people like you. Hire people who follow the rules. Another way to find these people is to look to see that they have good credit. You do not want any risk takers. Look for people with longevity in their job, in their marriage, and in their community.

"I've found that women and corporate dropouts make the best franchisees. Women make outstanding franchisees because they do what they're told, plus they're well organized, more motivated, and better at supervising and training. Corporate dropouts share many of those same characteristics. These are not the risk-takers, which makes them ideal franchisees. Also, many corporate dropouts have a significant golden parachute so financing is not a problem. In fact, a lot of these people will pay in cash.

"Above all, you need to find people with a lot of energy. You can't have franchisees who wear down at five or six o'clock because they need to keep going to nine or ten at night, six to seven days a week."

From an insider's perspective, the overriding concern involved control of franchisees, and a budding franchisor would do
well to recruit "rule-takers" and followers rather than "risk-
takers." This concern also played to the greatest fear an entre-
preneur-turned-franchisor was likely to have, that a franchisee
would take an enormous and useless risk to the detriment of,
and possible peril to, other franchisees in the system. This fear
was not totally unreasonable. Entrepreneurs franchise their
business to be able to provide the consistent delivery of a service or product across many locations. Any person who entered
a franchise system and began to tinker with the standard operating procedures threatened the consistency of the system.
But, more important, franchisees who deviated from the franchisor's methods directly questioned the authority, expertise,
and knowledge of the franchisor to claim that the standard operating procedures were the best way to operate the business.
Franchise consultants, like the one mentioned earlier, advised
their clients to seek franchisees who fit the above profile so that
the hallmark of franchising, consistent delivery of products and
services, could continue unabated.

One such type that fit the profile was so common within
the ranks of franchisees that insiders just referred to them as
"mom-and-pops." As a noted franchise consultant remarked,
"Mom-and-pop franchisees are used to working for someone,
and usually find it easy and natural to follow a franchisor's lead;
they usually come into a particular franchise without experience
in that type of business, and therefore without preconceived
notions of how the business should be run; and, after investing
their savings and futures in the outlet, mom-and-pops are likely
to work long and hard to make the business work."[1]

While the mom-and-pop franchisees appeared to be ideal re-
cruits from a franchisor's perspective, there were several drawbacks. Typically they lacked sophistication and capital, and they
often required greater supervision.[2] Consequently, franchisors

1. Donald D. Boroian and Patrick J. Boroian, *The Franchise Advantage: Make It Work for You* (Chicago: Prism Creative Group, 1987), 180.

2. Boroian and Boroian, 180.

were primarily encouraged to recruit corporate dropouts, women, and others who tend to follow the rules. At all costs, franchisors were encouraged to steer clear from the person who
"buys himself a job he can't be fired from." This was the person
who, upon entering into the security of a long-term contract,
merely operated the unit at some safe level or worse, regressed
toward the lower end of the sales and profitability spectrums.

The term "bought yourself a job" was a derogatory one from
both the franchisor's and franchisee's perspective. One franchisee from King Cleaners stated quite plainly, "If you're not
growing your business, then you bought yourself a job." Given
the choice between an entrepreneur who pushed the limits of
the system and the person who sought the security of a franchise system but not the risk associated with growth, franchisors
would do well to opt for the former.

From the insider's perspective, franchising attracted only two
types of franchisee, the person who would grow their business
and the person who would not. Of those that grew their business, they either did so within the stipulations of the given
franchise system and in accordance with the standard operating
procedures, or they did so outside of or without regard for the
standard guidelines of the system. But curiously, the profile of
franchisees from the insider's perspective was primarily a profile for prospective franchisees and not for existing franchisees.

This focus on prospective franchisees obviously points to one
of the key problems franchisors face; namely, the recruitment of
franchisees. A good deal of energy was spent by franchisors trying to identify the appropriate persons to buy franchises. Some
of those potential franchisees would be at the franchise expo.
Although it may be interesting to ponder the people at the expo
dashing from one franchise exhibit to the next, their arms full of
plastic bags touting the latest and greatest of franchise concepts
("Finally! A chicken franchise *you* can afford!!"), somehow a profile must be more thoughtful than the cryptic "this guy bought
himself a job."

It would seem a profile should say something about the people who make their livelihood as franchisees. Accordingly, I

developed a typology of franchisees that includes three generic profiles, what I term neo-franchisees, disillusioned, and side-liners.

I have stumped John, the master distributor for King Cleaners, with a simple question.

"Why do you think Rusty bought a franchise?"

"Whew, that's a good question," he responded. "If I knew the answer to that I'd go out and get a bunch more like him, but I've been scratching my head trying to figure that out ever since he got here. I have no idea."

We were in John's office located in an industrial park on the outskirts of the city. John's office was a hub of activity, but his own personal space was a sanctuary and was quite plain and ordinary. He had only one item on the wall, a framed biblical quote: "Be strong and of good courage, and do it. Fear not, be not dismayed; for the Lord God, even my God, is with you. He will not fail you or forsake you, until all the work for the service of the house of the Lord is finished" (1 Chron. 20:28). John, who was in his early 50s, operated his business with his wife Barbara and their son, Matt. They had built a very strong operation and were respected throughout the company by corporate executives and by other franchisees. As the master distributor for King Cleaners, John was responsible for the growth of franchise operations within his area, a large area extending from Lake Michigan to the Mississippi River and from Wisconsin two hundred miles south into Illinois.

John had several options for developing this area. He could sell new franchises, sell additional licenses to existing franchisees, or devise ways for current franchisees to increase their sales. Since John carried out multiple roles (trainer, marketer, inventory controller), his office served several functions. It was a warehouse, a training center, a place to meet with prospective franchisees, and it was subject to impromptu visits from King Cleaners executives who wanted to keep abreast of developments in the franchise system. As the distributor, John had a mediating role, one of liaison between the franchisees in his territory and "Central," but he was not a member of the corporate staff. Having purchased the rights to the territory, he was in the same relative position vis-à-vis the corporation as franchisees. He was similarly charged with growing the operations but had additional responsibilities, to develop franchisees and ensure that the quality standards of King Cleaners were met. In a short time, he had grown his area fourfold and had gained the trust and credibility of franchisees and corporate executives alike.

All franchisees in the area must eventually make their way to his warehouse to pick up supplies, and during these encounters John counseled franchisees who needed help, encouraged those who required it, and disciplined those who had stepped out of line. He was privy to nearly every deal that took place, knew the personal and professional issues franchisees were dealing with, and understood franchising better than most others at King Cleaners. But despite his years of experience and knowledge, it was the entry of Rusty into his system that had him baffled.

"We all sit around and discuss it, and none of us can figure out why he came to King Cleaners, and especially why he bought an existing franchise unit—he had virtually no leverage in that unit. He paid $250,000 for it, $125,000 in cash and the other half financed through the owner. But he's a real mover; he paid that off within two years. The way he sells, he could have built a business from scratch to the biggest in the system. But he keeps me moving. I'll tell you one thing, it sure has changed my life."

"What do you mean?" I asked.

"Ho, boy! He's a real go-getter. He calls in every day, and he expects to be put right through." He leaned forward in his desk, raised his voice, and spoke to Barbara. "Isn't that right?"

"Oh," she laughed, "that's an understatement. He calls in at least two or three times a day."

"And he's always working on deals," John continued. "He's got big, big plans for his business. In fact, he's already won every award you can win—fastest-growing franchise, highest revenue in the shortest time span, and a couple other awards . . . "

"He missed one," Barbara interrupted, "the fastest to a million in revenues, I think."

"Oh, yeah. He missed that one because he didn't have a new franchise, but an existing one. So he lost on a technicality, and he was pretty mad about it. He wanted to win every award."

"Doesn't everybody want to win the awards?" I asked.

"You'd think so, but there are a lot of people that are satisfied staying at a certain level. Anyway, you'll have to meet Rusty, and then you can decide for yourself what I mean. I'm sure he'd like to speak with you."

So I met Rusty the following week at his office in an outlying suburb. Similar to John's office, Rusty had a small building in an industrial park with a front office, a meeting room in the center, and a shop in the back for supplies and repair of equipment. In the meeting room were a television and a man in his early twenties watching a King Cleaners video on cleaning.

Rusty greeted me in the front office, and as we passed through the meeting room he said, "That's a job applicant there." He then turned to the fellow and asked, "How's it going?" As we continued to his office he said, "You know that in our business nearly all of the employees are part-time, and most of them don't speak any English at all. I have all prospective employees watch the video. It introduces them to the company and what we do, but it also is a great tool for finding out who will be a good worker. I figure if a guy will watch something as boring as a King Cleaners video on cleaning for an hour, he'll find working for me a joy."

Rusty's recruiting approach, like most of the things about him, was unconventional—at least by King Cleaners standards. Although Rusty was in his early forties, about the same age as many of the other franchisees, that was about the only characteristic he had in common with them. Unlike the other franchisees, Rusty had a nicely appointed office, wore a Rolex watch, drove a sports car, belonged to an upscale country club, was part-owner of a corporate jet, and had aggressive goals for his business. He also had an MBA from one of the top programs in the country and had fairly extensive experience as a business executive with several Fortune 500 companies.

"Let me start with an easy question," I began. "Why did you buy a franchise?"

Without hesitating Rusty smiled and replied, "[T]o make a lot of money." Surprisingly, he was the only person at King Cleaners that had that response.

"But why did you buy a King Cleaners franchise?" I asked.

"To make a lot of money," he reaffirmed. "I was familiar with King Cleaners, I had business dealings with them as an executive in my previous job, and I thought I could make a lot of money here. I had a golden parachute, and I didn't want to work for anyone. I had headhunters tell me that I could not survive in the corporate world, that my personality and drive would clash. I'm too independent for the corporate world, so I knew I'd have to do something else. I'm a fanatic on cleanliness and this is a good service business."

"So, how has your experience been here?" I asked.

"Well, the business part of it is fine. I've achieved nearly all of my goals. I've paid off my loan to the previous owner early—it was a five-year loan and I paid it off in two years. I have been able to increase my contribution—you know that's an internal measure of profitability that King Cleaners uses?"

"Yeah, I've heard people talk about that term."

"OK. Anyway, I increased my contribution to King Cleaners from 38 percent, which is high, to 44 percent. King Cleaners expects a 30 percent contribution, so nobody thought I should buy an existing franchise that had such a high contribution. They thought it would go down, maybe they even hoped that it would go down, you never know. Even John told me to buy a new one, but I knew the business was undervalued so it was a good deal. But I tell you, I don't have a high opinion of the corporate executives. I get along fine with John, but these corporate guys are a bunch of amateurs! They're just not very smart. Do you know that I bought the rights to Cuba? They laughed at me when I said I wanted them. They thought I was crazy and sold me the rights for six thousand dollars. That's it! Six thousand dollars! Castro is going to fall sometime in my lifetime, and I'll be there the day after he dies. Cuba has the most beautiful beaches in the world, and Havana is lined with hotels. All those businesses have to be cleaned, and I'll be the only one with the rights to develop it under the King Cleaners trademark. But these guys were not smart enough to recognize that.

"They really don't know what they're doing. They wear their blue blazers—I mean, come on! This is not the 1950s anymore, and we're not IBM, anyway. They only know one thing, and that's cleaning. They're all inbred. There's not a guy in that executive group that has any experience in any industry outside of cleaning. Not one. And the worst part is I compete with them. I bought the rights to another town because it has so many office buildings. One company has over three million square feet and that would be a huge account to land. Anyway, I told John, 'By God, you're not selling any more licenses in my area' and so far he hasn't. But I'm not only competing with other franchisees, I have to compete with King Cleaners. They've got their own corporate cleaning services, and they have sales reps trying to land the big commercial accounts. Then they turn around and subcontract that out to the franchise guys. Well, screw that! I can do the whole thing myself. I don't mind competing for a job, but I don't want to compete with my own company."

Neo-franchisees, like Rusty, were outspoken critics of the franchisor and with good reason: most neo-franchisees were successful in the business. In fact, several of the neo-franchisees at Sign Masters knew the business better than did the founder Stu Beyer. And at Star Muffler, the entire program was based upon the operations of Pete Morgan, one of the early franchisees. Rusty had figured out a clever way to increase his profits considerably by selling "special" cleaning services to clients, a service that did not require special skills or unique equipment.

"I always schedule special projects routinely into the contract," Rusty explained, "and perform them on a monthly basis. I don't bid it that way, I bid it at the normal charge, but on the monthly bill I charge for the special projects."

"But what if they complain? What if they decide that you're over-charging?" I asked.

"I tell them what it's for. I mean, I give them an itemized bill."

"No, I mean what if they only want the basic spot-vac service?"

"Oh, yeah, some people complain but I ask them, 'Do you want coffee stains on the carpet? Because eventually the carpet will get worn in those spots and you'll have to replace the whole thing.' Listen, I'm not selling them something they don't need. And let's face it, this is a lot cheaper than replacing the whole carpet. They always come around because it makes good business sense to do the preventative maintenance."

Paradoxically, neo-franchisees were outspoken critics but were also open-minded about the business. I found that most neo-franchisees were often the first ones to try new approaches and that they usually embraced the promotional programs franchisors set up. They also had a better grasp of the franchisee-franchisor relationship, especially the limits of the relationship. For instance, one franchisee from King Cleaners stated, "King Cleaners get their money from my sales. They want to find things they can sell me, because it's their name and my market. But If I go out tomorrow, they don't lose much. They have no stake whether I make a profit or not. Their only stake is in my continuing revenues and product sales. Most people lose sight of that fact." Indeed, one of the defining characteristics of neo-franchisees is the realization that they are but a small part of a system, that their business—no matter how big—is relatively unimportant to the franchisor. Like Rusty, neo-franchisees realize that their profitability is up to them to achieve.

While other franchisees complained that the trademark only helped them get in the door to speak with clients, Rusty exclaimed, "What more do you need? In this business, that should be enough to make the sale. Most of these guys are asking for a free ride. They bought the franchise thinking King Cleaners would do all the work for them, but they only bought the right to operate under the King Cleaners trademark and the opportunity to have King Cleaners tell them how to run the business. I think that many of the franchisee problems come from not following the King Cleaners 'plan.' They tell you to keep your capital outlay down to about 5 percent of your gross billing because if it's anything more it's hard to break even. I keep mine down to 3 percent, but a lot of these guys go way, way beyond this. Then they wonder why they're not making any money!"

But neo-franchisee openness and willingness to go along with the franchisor only went so far. One franchisee at Sign Masters installed a photocopy machine in his store because he found that customers asked him to make copies. When the field man for Sign Masters came in to his store he said to the franchisee, "You know you have to pay a royalty on all the money you get from the photocopy machine, right?" The franchisee responded, "Yeah." But later, to me he said, "I put the photocopy machine in myself. I paid for it with my own money. I'm not paying a royalty to them on that! They hadn't even thought of a photocopier until I did it. How is that a part of the trademark?" Rusty once told me about a situation he had with John, indicating just how far he was willing to be pushed by the franchisor.

"We were at a meeting, a conference, in California, and John took out to dinner all the franchisees in his territory, probably about thirty guys. Well, anyway, we were at a very nice restaurant, and I order a Scotch and water. I waited a long time and finally the waitress comes back to the room but she doesn't have my drink. So I ask her about it and she says, 'I can't bring you one.' So I think, OK, maybe in a little while after she gets all the orders in. When she comes back a second time, I ask her again about the drink and she says she *won't* bring me one. 'What do you mean,' I say, 'is the bar closed?' And she says, 'Oh, no, the bar's open, but your group does not get any alcoholic beverages.' And I say, 'Excuse me? What does that mean?' and she tells me that our group is not supposed to have any drinks. Well, I said, 'The hell with that,' so I got up and went to the bar and bought two scotch and waters and brought them back to my seat, next to John. You know, John's a religious guy and doesn't drink at all. Of course, everyone in the room stared at me like I was crazy, but it's my dinner and I want a Scotch and water with it, and neither John nor anyone else is going to tell me what to do. If it is something to do with the franchise, then fine, I'll listen, but they can't tell me how to run my life."

Not all neo-franchisees had as militant an attitude as Rusty, but they did have an aggressive and confident approach to their business and were more sophisticated than others in the system. Part of this sophistication and confidence was due to their education, for neo-franchisees tended to be better educated than others. Many had college degrees in technical fields like engineering and chemistry, and some had earned an MBA. Part of their self-confidence was also due to a track record of success in prior careers. The term "corporate drop-out" was not a completely descriptive term. Although many neo-franchisees entered franchising from the managerial and executive ranks of corporate America, many had careers as teachers and airline pilots as well as in government agencies and the military. The move into franchising represented a major career change, since none of these franchisees had previously owned a business and none had prior experience in the industry.

Nevertheless, neo-franchisees had full confidence in their abilities and had no doubts that they would be successful as franchisees. The rhetoric that franchise systems had a "higher success rate" than other business forms was never a part of the decision process to enter franchising in the first place, and it had no bearing on whether or not the neo-franchisee would succeed. As an example of the confidence typical of neo-franchisees, several Sign Masters franchisees mentioned that even though they anticipated the eventual collapse and bankruptcy of the company, they still expected their business to be operating. The idea that the firm might become insolvent caused considerable angst among the other Sign Masters franchisees but was of minor consequence, an annoyance or distraction at most, to the neo-franchisees.

Perhaps the defining characteristic of neo-franchisees was the financial capital they brought into the system and the return they made on their investment. Neo-franchisees typically were the top performers in any franchise system, and they had commensurately high incomes. But it was their capital reserves, their financial muscle, that separated them from other franchisees: Nearly all of the neo-franchisees had the financial means and wherewithal to overcome nearly any obstacle that might arise to threaten their business. For instance, although Rusty spent nearly $250,000 out of his pocket to buy his franchise unit, the purchase depleted under 25 percent of his available resources. Few other franchisees had the financial means to purchase a franchise of that size, no matter how it would be financed. For neo-franchisees, the extensive capital reserves meant that they had the ability and means to flee the system at any time, and they could go on to dabble in other occupations or pursue other opportunities if they so desired. It was the safety valve of capital reserves that allowed neo-franchisees to go along with new ideas and programs of the franchisor. Neo-franchisees gave the firm the benefit of the doubt and were generally more trusting of corporate members. It was also the case that neo-franchisees, because of their extensive business experience and success in the system, were more likely to want to impart that knowledge to others in the system. When I asked franchisees if they would ever want to work on the franchisor side of the business, neo-franchisees were likely to respond, "Sure. I think I could help them."

The view of other franchisees and corporate managers toward the neo-franchisees was similarly positive: neo-franchisees were the most respected and trusted franchisees in the system. They were also monitored at a rate far below that of other franchisees and were given greater license to do things within the system. At King Cleaners, territorial disputes among franchisees were common and a major source of friction, but Rusty said, "John told me I could go wherever I want." At Star Muffler, Pete Morgan stated, "These guys really don't bother me much. I can't tell you the last time they were in my store. I still have a sign from ten years ago." The trust of neo-franchisees was probably well deserved. I asked one franchisee if it was possible to cheat, to underreport income. He replied, "Sure. I could cheat and they couldn't catch me. But why would I do that? Why would I risk losing something worth one hundred thousand dollars for a thousand bucks a month?"

## DISILLUSIONED FRANCHISEES

"You should change your study," Tom, a franchisee with King Cleaners told me. "You should study people over a longer period of time to figure out when they get it."

"Get what?" I asked.

"You know, when they figure it out, when they finally figure out what franchising is like. I don't know. I think it would be interesting to see when the honeymoon period wears off for people."

"When did it wear off for you?"

"I'm not sure. It took me a couple of years. I was pretty naive. I mean, I really believed King Cleaners. I like and agree with their values, and I especially liked John. He was kind of like a father figure to me, and he always seemed so helpful."

"Well," I asked, "how did things change? Are the values now the same as when you started?"

"Yeah, but I don't believe they follow them that closely. I always heard, no—I was told—that King Cleaners doesn't make any money off of products, that they sell everything to us at cost so we can be more competitive. But I have two different distributors that I buy products from, one in Minneapolis and one in Chicago. The prices are not the same for the same products; sometimes they differ a lot. I figure if the distributors are making money on product, so is King Cleaners."[When I asked John about this, he sheepishly responded, "Well, we're supposed to sell the products at the same price. We don't make much money on products, though."] Anyway, I don't know. I used to be passionate about owning this franchise and growing it, but now, well, I don't know."

"Why don't you leave?"

"Oh, well, I've got a mortgage, kids, I don't think I could leave now."

"It sounds like you have regrets."

"Yeah, in some respects I do. I know now why John sold me this franchise. Actually, he convinced me to buy the franchise. At the time, I was a supervisor in the franchise, and my boss was going through a divorce and wanted to sell. Well, during the six months from the time I bought the franchise to the time I actually gained control my boss had lost a lot of accounts, he just sort of let them fall by the wayside. So I overpaid for the franchise. I understand why John convinced me to buy. Who else would buy into a small market? He wanted the revenue. He got a good guy in there, and he didn't have to pay for any training since I already knew a lot about the business. John has a way of getting you to do something that is not really in your best interests. It is in his best interests, but not really in yours."

Disillusioned franchisees largely believe that buying a franchise was the worst decision they ever made. Fortunately, they were relatively young—mostly in their thirties—so the chance to recover and embark on a new career was higher than for others in the system. But while in the system, disillusioned franchisees harbored ill will toward the franchisor and other franchisees, and they were convinced that they received a "raw deal" from the franchisor even if the facts did not bear them out. For instance, one Star Muffler franchisee paid the lowest price (by about sixty thousand dollars) of any person to enter the franchise system, and chief executive officer Mark Spinelli said, "He got a very good deal. We bent over backwards to give him all sorts of advantages. We gave him a low-interest loan, we let him have the equipment. Charlie Lafer doesn't know what a good deal he got." But Charlie said to me, "They sold me a loser store. They couldn't sell it for ten years. In 1988, it lost over seventy thousand dollars, and it's still losing money. It's a loser location."

Another disillusioned franchisee at King Cleaners told me how he was fooled into "giving away" his business. "Originally I bought a small business license," he explained, "one that lets me contract to businesses under five thousand square feet. As it turns out I was the first one to get that type of license—the first one in the entire company, and I spent a lot of time and effort into learning about this market. I mean, *a lot* of time learning about the market, and I built up a pretty good business. You can make a ton of money in this market, you know, it only takes one employee a couple hours two times a week to clean a building. So your costs are like fifty bucks a week—tops— and you charge a hundred bucks. And you don't have to deal with any contract managers, and there's a lot less competition— only against the mom-and-pops—and we can beat them every time. Anyway, after I get this going, it turns out that a secretary in John's office wanted to get into a King Cleaners business, and John talked me into selling her my license and buying a commercial license. Basically, they screwed me over. They saw a way to profit and convinced me that it was in my best interests to sell. But I gave away my business. It was a good deal for her, a great deal, but it was lousy for me. Now I have a commercial license in the most crowded market—I'm right in the middle of the two biggest guys, and I'm not going to make anything. They screwed me over big time."

Another disillusioned franchisee from Star Muffler regret- ted buying a franchise soon after he opened his store. "Their 'turnkey' operation is a joke," he said. "They turn the key and leave you to teach yourself. I'm not kidding. I had to call a com- petitor down the street and ask him, 'How do I do this?' and 'What do I price this at?' If he hadn't helped me, I wouldn't have made it. I don't know what it's like for the new guys now, but I tell everybody that I got put into business by my Goddamned competitor!"

This feeling of regret, of having made a big mistake, was com- pounded by the high cost disillusioned franchisees had paid to enter the system. Unlike neo-franchisees that had large capi- tal reserves, disillusioned franchisees had virtually no reserves, having spent all of their money to enter. Many borrowed from their parents or relatives, some used inheritance money or took out a second mortgage on their home. In short, they used every means available. As one franchisee stated, "I begged, borrowed, and stole to get in here."

For disillusioned franchisees, the pressure to perform was high, and their own expectations were high. The reality, however, was that they were not among the top performers in the system, and they were not making the kind of money they envisioned when they started out. I asked one franchisee, a personal friend of Stu Beyer's, how much money he was making, and he startled me with his blunt response: "Not a fucking thing." Yet, when I asked disillusioned franchisees why they couldn't get their business up to the desired levels, they invoked all sorts of excuses. "The franchisor does not understand my market," or, "The company is focusing all their marketing efforts toward the suburbs and that doesn't work in a small market." One often heard, "My customers are different."

Although disillusioned franchisees rarely (if ever) blamed themselves for their plight, that was squarely where franchisors placed the blame. John, from King Cleaners, said about Tom, "He's a dreamer. He doesn't know what's good for himself. He's always looking to do something else. He should just buckle down, work at his own job, and take on his competition there in his town." One long-time franchisor for King Cleaners stated, "Most of the guys that come into the franchise are young guys who couldn't make it in the corporate world. They think that the reason they didn't make it was because they were held back or because someone held a grudge against them. But when they don't make it in franchising, they learn a tough lesson. They learn that it was them all along, and the reason they didn't make it was because they weren't good enough. And that's a tough lesson to learn, especially when you're a young guy."

On the way to learning that tough lesson, disillusioned franchisees became the malcontents of the system, and they made that known to everyone they interacted with. They harbored a skepticism and cynicism about franchising and directed their anger toward the franchisor. Part of the skepticism derived from the very innocence that led the disillusioned franchisees into franchising in the first place: most of them believed the rhetoric that franchise units had a better success rate. Equally, they learned that any modest success they achieved was due to their own hard work and perseverance. As one franchisee commented, "Every lead I ever got (from the franchisor) I paid for. Every one."

Disillusioned franchisees had entered into franchising believing that the products the franchisor provided were both superior and cheaper than what one could find otherwise. As a Star Muffler franchisee said, "The products are all the same. It doesn't matter who you buy from, and I gotta think that if you owned your own shop, you'd get the same deal we get. I mean, the distributor is out here anyway, why wouldn't he deliver product to the independent guy for the same price?"

A King Cleaners franchisee stated, "I used to buy the company line, you know, 'These are the best products, we're working hard for you, we want you to be successful, we're only as successful as the franchisees.' They want you to think that King Cleaners is the best company in the world. Well, I don't buy that line anymore. Their products are not superior, but weak. I don't even use the products in my own home. They keep their products weak so the products can't do much damage."

In addition, the rhetoric about being your own boss ("Work *for* yourself not *by* yourself!") was quickly dispelled as the disillusioned franchisee learned that franchising affords almost no independence for franchisees and no tolerance on the part of the franchisor for persons that want to operate independently. Disillusioned franchisees had an experience in franchising that differed drastically from what they expected, from the amount of help they would receive from the franchisor to the number of customers they would have and the return they would be earning. Many of them assumed that they would be managing a profitable operation almost immediately, but they found that they were carrying out multiple tasks and that they had to "do everything" to make a meager profit.

On top of that, one key to success as a franchisee meant being a great salesperson. As one disillusioned franchisee stated, "Sales is 99, no, 100 percent of owning a franchise. That's all we do, and if you can't sell, then you're not in business."

But the anger of disillusioned franchisees was not limited to franchisors. It also extended to others in the system, especially the high-performing franchisees. At a meeting among Star Muffler franchisees on the executive board, one franchisee complained to Pete Morgan, the top producer: "Hell, if I had all the Cadillacs and Lincolns that you had, I'd be making a lot, too."

Pete Morgan chuckled. "I don't have any more guys with Cadillacs and Lincolns than you do."

"Christ! That's fucking bullshit," the other guy countered.

This animosity toward the top performers was displayed in front of chief executive officer Mark Spinelli. That's why I was surprised when he told me sometime later that during an annual meeting he had Pete Morgan give a talk to the other guys about some of the things he was doing in his shop. Understandably, the animosity arose again.

"I thought he would be able to get through to these guys since he was a franchisee," Spinelli stated. "They don't listen to us. They shut us down the minute we start telling them something. So we brought in Pete Morgan, and it was awful."

"What, he's a bad speaker?" I asked.

"No, he had to quit early because they were so brutal to him. They just killed the guy. They really dragged him through the wringer. It was a harrowing experience. I'll never do that again, never put a franchisee in the position of being ridiculed and criticized in front of others."

"What part of it didn't they believe?"

"These guys want to blame somebody for their problems, and usually it's us. But this time they took it out on Morgan."

At King Cleaners, the top performers were not criticized openly, but only privately. One of the disillusioned franchisees said about Rusty, "Man, that guy can sell sand to the Saudis. But that's all he can do. If he didn't have all that money coming in, if he had my debt, he wouldn't be doing half as well as me."

"Well, suppose you had his money, what would you do?" I asked.

"Well . . . ah . . . "

He stammered and thought for a little bit. "I'd . . . ah . . . I'd run a really big marketing campaign, send out postcards to all the businesses in the area."

This was a pretty feeble response. King Cleaners already marketed heavily nationally, regionally, and locally, and the company was widely known in the area in which the disillusioned franchisee operated. Fifty thousand dollars of marketing would do little to help him. But it was a lot easier to look at the top performers and assume that their success was due to something "lucky" like capital reserves, while one's own failure was blamed on the "market."

The disillusioned franchisees are caught in a difficult bind, for they are hard-pressed financially and somewhat unwilling to take responsibility for their franchise. One solution was to take liberties with the franchise, to take shortcuts wherever one could. As one franchisee stated, "You got to make a profit any way you can, and if it means cutting corners, then we cut corners. I specifically bid a job with the idea in mind that the workers will get faster by 20 percent. There are also things you can do on the books, underreport and stuff. I think everyone does that to some extent."

One such franchisee at King Cleaners who did so was Scott, a twenty-five-year-old former Marine. Scott was the franchisee mentioned earlier who bought a small business license, sold it back to John ("gave it away"), and now had a license in a congested market. He was ill-suited to business ownership and did not hold the values of King Cleaners. He had a disagreeable disposition and outlook, which carried over to others in the system, especially his employees.

"You know," he said as we were driving to a job site, "guys like 'X' and 'Y' (his two main King Cleaners competitors) are only doing well because they can exploit a minority (Hispanic) labor market. I take that back. 'X' has his Dad helping him, working in the back fixing equipment and stuff. That helps a lot. I'm here all by myself. If something breaks down, I have to fix it. I have to do the marketing, I have to do the selling, I have to supervise the employees. Both those guys have all sorts of help. It's really hard to do by yourself. Impossible. But they also exploit the minority pool. That's the only way you can do it. But I can't get any Hispanics to work for me, I mean, between the two of them they have about 150 workers. I'm experimenting with the Ethiopian labor market."

"The Ethiopian labor market?" I asked in a perplexed voice.

"Yeah, there's a bunch of them that go to the local college here, so I hired a couple of them, well, actually only one, and he had a brother, a couple of sisters, and cousins. They all live in the same house just off campus. See, in order to make the most money, you need a building large enough to have four workers, and only one of them has to be able to speak English."

We arrived at the building, a relatively small warehouse, at around midnight. Inside were three of the workers, all in their late teens or early twenties. They became agitated by Scott's presence and immediately scattered to various parts of the building. Scott checked the supplies in the closet, dropped off a few cleaning towels, and picked up a pile of dirty ones.

"Where's Rashdi?" he asked.

One of the workers, Rashdi's brother, mumbled something.

"Where's Rashdi? Where's Rashdi? Do you know where he is?" Scott asked, raising his voice angrily. "Why isn't he here?"

The worker cowered and mumbled again. Although the man understood little English, Scott's demeanor and body language clarified the situation.

Scott again screamed to the worker, "Where's Rashdi? Where's Rashdi? Do you know where he is? Why isn't he here?"

"Rashdi no good," he replied.

"What?! Is he sick? Is Rashdi sick? Where is he?"

The worker pointed to his teeth. "Rashdi no good," he replied again.

"He's at the dentist? No, it's fucking midnight, he's not at the dentist." Scott hesitated for a moment. "Rashdi's sick from the dentist? Why didn't he call me? Where is he now, is he at home?"

The worker shook his head. Scott stormed out of the main area to a phone in a nearby office and called Rashdi's house. "Where's Rashdi?" he barked into the phone. "Why isn't he here? Let me talk to Rashdi. Go get him." Rashdi did not answer the phone, and Scott became angrier still. He gave the phone to Rashdi's brother. "You talk to Rashdi and get him here. I want to know why he didn't call me." The brother spoke on the phone to Rashdi and after a short while said to Scott, "Rashdi no good. He not coming."

"OK, fine. You have to do the work for him."

"No, too much."

"Yes. You knew that Rashdi was sick, you knew that he wasn't coming tonight."

"But I come to work, I here," he protested.

"I don't care. You have to finish his work for him. And you have to do it at your pay scale. I'm not paying you to finish Rashdi's work."

As we drove to the next job site, I asked Scott how much longer he planned to own his franchise, and he angrily replied, "Not one Goddamn minute longer than I have to. I used to worry about this shit. When a client would call up that something wasn't right, I'd go right over there and take care of it myself. Everyone thinks they're a fucking Demming, and that the quality has to be at his level. Well, I'm not going to be Mr. Quality anymore. Now, if I get a call or a client threatens me that they're going to close the account, I just go home and watch TV."

That would be fine by everybody else at King Cleaners. Although not too numerous, disillusioned franchisees were well known by others in the system. They were neither respected nor trusted by others and, like Scott, were awkward to deal with or be around. Similarly, while franchisors appreciated the relatively high sales of the disillusioned franchisees, they tired of their incessant negative attitudes. As Stu Beyer of Sign Masters stated, "For some of these guys, nothing is right. If it's so bad, why don't they just leave?"

Many would like to, but there were hurdles to leaving. One was financial. With all their resources tied to the franchise unit, disillusioned franchisees were constantly striving to "make it," to at least break even and recoup their investment. Another hurdle was experience. Unlike neo-franchisees, who had wide-ranging work experiences, disillusioned franchisees had a career that was tied up solely in the franchise system or to some other career that was equally unattractive, such as a beer truck driver. This limited their ability to move to something different.

So while it might appear that the disillusioned franchisees had many other career opportunities or alternatives as a result of their relative youth, in fact they had few. This led one franchisee to comment, "They got me right where I don't want to be."

SIDELINERS

Another group, sideliners, was marginal to franchising, not in terms of sales, but in terms of the network of relationships that enmeshed others. While sideliners lacked the confidence and assertiveness of the neo-franchisees and the abrasiveness of disillusioned franchisees, they were in some respects the stable backbone of the system. Sideliners were distinct because of their ordinariness: they were less involved with others in the system, kept to themselves, were quiet, did not complain, and expected little from the franchisor. And that was the way they preferred it to be. One sideliner said to me, "I want the franchisor to leave me alone. That's why I'm happy when a new guy comes in because that's one more person to keep the franchisor off my back."

Neo-franchisees and disillusioned franchisees knew about sideliners, but they were not counted as people one had to contend with in order to get the attention of the franchisor. They were observers rather than players in the system. Sideliners, as the term implies, were not only marginalized in terms of their social relationships but also on a number of characteristics—minorities, women, franchisees distant from company headquarters, the oldest franchisees, those with the least experience, and persons who were relatively obscure and unknown by other franchisees. Despite their somewhat pedestrian qualities, sideliners could have high sales and some had extensive experience in franchising.

Sideliners were almost resigned to the fact that they would be somewhat marginal to the company, and they seemed to be content to just get by. One sideliner said to me, "I really am not all that interested in growing the business. I'd be happy to make $45,000 a year." Another stated, "Yeah, you can grow the business, but growth also brings problems. I'd just as soon stay at my current level." One King Cleaners sideliner said, "I'm not like those other guys in the system, working sixty, maybe even eighty hours a week. I basically go to bed around ten at night and sleep in until nine in the morning, and I don't take any calls outside of normal business hours—none. I figure nothing can be that urgent that it needs my immediate attention. The franchisor is always getting at me to increase my sales, but for what? I'm doing OK the way things are now."

Sideliners were not difficult to manage compared to neo-franchisees and disillusioned franchisees, but they required an enormous amount of coaching by franchisors, who constantly implored them to increase sales. The sideliners I worked with did not know much about the franchise system, were not entirely clear on who was who, and were generally quite distant from all others and the daily trappings of the company. Sign Masters had a large contingent of sideliners, enough for Stu Beyer to raise his hands in exasperation, "For some of these guys 'growth' is a dirty word. They just will not grow their business."

Sideliners did not differ all that much from neo-franchisees in terms of career experience, and many sideliners had had corporate careers, were teachers, or had some other professional career. They lacked the capital reserves of neo-franchisees, but they also did not spend all of their reserves like the disillusioned franchisees. However, there were vast differences in outlook between these three types of franchisee.

Neo-franchisees had high expectations that were generally met. I once asked Rusty, from King Cleaners, how often he spoke with John.

"Every day," he replied.

"He calls you every day?" I asked.

"No, I call him every day. Hey, I don't work for King Cleaners. King Cleaners works for me! They had better answer my calls."

It was this expectation on the part of the neo-franchisee and their delivery on that expectation that was both exciting for franchisors but quite taxing of the latter's time and organizational resources. Disillusioned franchisees, by contrast, had high expectations that went unmet. Unfortunately, the franchisor also had high expectations. In fact, it was the very characteristics of young age and aggressive attitude that drew franchisors to disillusioned franchisees in the first place, but those characteristics, coupled with an unrealistic perspective on what could be accomplished within a franchise system, fueled the ultimate disenchantment of disillusioned franchisees. Sideliners differed from both neo-franchisees and disillusioned franchisees in one important respect: They did not have high expectations of themselves or their franchise unit. They were content to get by, to grow their business at relatively conservative levels—if at all—and to remain observers of the franchise system.

## A SINGULAR PROFILE

Although I found three types of franchisees—neo-franchisees, disillusioned franchisees, and sideliners—there were common experiences and uncertainties that led franchisees to be more alike than dissimilar. For example, franchisees faced the same set of uncertainties with respect to the environment in which they operated. As small business owners they had similar labor woes, and they shared risks of operating on the periphery of the economy. These problems seemed inherent to franchising, and nearly all franchisees grappled with them on a daily basis, regardless of their profile.

Another element common across all three franchisee profiles was the sheer amount of hard work needed to keep a franchise unit profitable or even solvent. Franchisees expended an enormous amount of time and energy to keep everything going, and this effort was largely unnoticed by franchisors. One franchisee from Sign Masters stated, "The amount of administrative time is way more than I thought it would be. And it's not just taxes and record-keeping, but all sorts of forms and reports that Beyer has us fill out. The franchisor has no idea how much time it takes to fill out all these pointless forms they make us do."

Again, regardless of their profile, franchisees worked long hours, operated six or seven days a week, and rarely took vacations. But despite all the hard work, the returns were palpably low. At King Cleaners, franchisee incomes ranged from a low of zero to $125,000 but averaged under $30,000. At Sign Masters, the range was zero to $60,000 with most franchisees averaging $22,000. At Star Muffler, the income ranged from $25,000 to $125,000 but the average was $35,000. Given the amount of effort and returns franchisees can expect, it comes as no surprise that turnover rates within franchise systems can be quite high, as I pointed out in chapter 2. But yet there are franchisees who survive and prosper in the three companies discussed in the preceding chapters. What strategies do they use to do so? What factors influence franchisee performance?

# CHAPTER 7

NETWORKS, ALLIANCES,
AND SURVIVAL

Scott, from King Cleaners, and I had just finished checking a client site, and we headed out the door to his van through a driving rain. It was late, around 2 A.M., and we were done for the night. As we backed out Scott began to talk about his life.

"I didn't have much growing up, and from the earliest time I can remember I've been working. I never really expected to get to college so when I got out of high school I joined the Marines."

"How was that?"

"Not bad. Got to see the world a little bit. But I tell ya, being in the Marines can make you think about education, that's for sure. When I got out, I went to a local college. Majored in criminal justice. We didn't have any money, and I wouldn't have asked my parents for anything anyway, so I started working at King Cleaners, working for a franchisee who had some buildings to clean downtown."

"Who did you work for?"

"With Steve. He's not here anymore—he sold his business to Rusty. Anyway, it's not bad doing the work in this business. It takes a little effort, but you can basically do the work on your own time, you know, you do it when you want. As long as it's clean before the client shows up the next morning, you've got no problems. You got the key and the supplies and you just go in there and do your thing. Listen to a little music. Don't worry about much. Kinda even relaxes you to clean."

"Do you miss it?"

"Not the money, you make nothing. But, you know, there's no hassles. Don't have to do any fucking marketing, don't have to be Mr. Businessman, Mr. Sales. That's the thing I hate about this. Owning a business consumes me, consumes all of my time and energy. I mean, shit, it's two o'clock in the morning and I'm fucking driving around checking up on a bunch of Ethiopians. I should be fucking sleeping. Tomorrow I got a goddamned sales call at nine o'clock. I tell you one thing, though, I'm not doing this one goddamn minute longer than I have to."

"How long is that?"

"I applied to police officer school out in California. Actually, I got accepted just today. I want to be on the highway patrol. I don't ever want to think about marketing, or sales, or people being late, or people stealing from me or from clients—none of that crap—I don't ever want to even think about that shit again. I was naive when I bought this. I thought it'd be really cool to own my own business. Thought I'd make a ton of money by the time I'm thirty. Well, I'm twenty-seven and I'll be broke by the time I'm thirty."

Suddenly Scott slammed on the brakes, and we slid out of control. "Goddammit!" he yelled.

"What? Did we hit something?"

"No" he replied as he turned the van around. "Goddamn son of a bitch."

"What? What are you talking about? There's no one on the road—"

"I saw a goddamn King Cleaners van at the building down the street. And you know what? This is my territory. So if I'm driving my van then that van doesn't belong here, and I'm gonna find out who the fuck it is."

We pulled into the parking lot just as a franchisee was unloading some supplies from the van. I braced myself for the confrontation between Scott, the high-strung ex-Marine, and an unsuspecting franchisee.

"Hey," Scott called out as he rolled down his window, "you get a new van?"

"New to me. This is the one Rusty sold me. Why?"

"You fucking gave me a heart attack. I didn't recognize you and as we were driving by I saw a new van in the lot. I was coming over to bust somebody's balls."

"Nope. Just me."

"Yeah, OK. See ya later." As we drove off Scott turned to me and said, "No big deal. Just Chuck."

I knew Chuck, having worked with him a few months earlier. But I didn't know why Scott had dismissed his transgression so quickly.

"What's Chuck doing here?" I asked.

"Oh, see, me, Chuck, and Dan—you know Dan [the highest revenue franchisee])?"

"Yeah, I know him."

"Yeah, well, he approached me one day with a deal to form an alliance and split up the market. He'd take the big clients, Chuck, the medium-sized, and I get the small ones. We're all on top of each other here, I mean, Christ! There's probably fifteen guys within a ten mile radius of me. I'm right in the middle of where everyone wants to be, but Dan and Chuck are like, right here. It's not really good for the client to get sales calls from all these franchisees. So we split up the market."

"That's a medium size client? What's a small client?"

"No, that should be one of my accounts, but," Scott looked over at me and grinned, "I got some crap that should be his and I don't want to let him know about it. I'll let him keep that account. He probably didn't go after it, probably is part of another account he already has."

As we drove along, Scott finished his thoughts. "You see, you can't really own your own business. That's just bullshit King Cleaners promotes. Even Dan, you know, it looks like he's this lone cowboy working all these deals with these big corporations, but he's got his dad helping him, his wife helping him. I'm all by myself, and you just can't do it."

"Well, isn't that what King Cleaners says, 'Work for yourself, not by yourself?'"

"That's what I'm saying, but it's not King Cleaners that makes a difference. Shit, those guys only care about Dan and Rusty and a couple of other high rollers. A guy like me? They could care less. No, see, this alliance saved me. It's not King Cleaners but the other guys that make a difference. If Dan hadn't asked me to join in, I'd be out of business. I'm going out anyhow since I'm leaving, but this way I'll be able to get something for it—the license is worth something, worth more than a new license."

SOCIAL CAPITAL

Scott expressed a fundamental insight on franchising: his survival depended to a great extent on forming connections with others. Of course, the trademark, corporate training, marketing, and operations are important, but even more critical was his alliance with other franchisees, Chuck and Dan. But forming connections with others is a counterintuitive strategy for most franchisees to follow since they often equate franchising with entrepreneurship and entrepreneurship with individualism. Even so, the survival of franchisees hinges not solely upon their individual efforts but also upon their ability to create and foster relationships with others in their system. This connection with others is a form of capital, "social capital," and it is an important property of social life. In fact, the character, frequency, strength, and pattern of connection among franchise participants impacts their ability to survive and profit in the system.

And survival within a franchise system is not a forgone conclusion. In chapter 2, I pointed out that the turnover rates for franchisees range from 9 percent at Star Muffler to 35 percent at King Cleaners and 24 percent at Sign Masters. Although these percentages are high, there are also people that not only survive, but thrive within franchising. What explains a franchisee's ability to survive or even profit, as Pete Morgan at Star Muffler and Rusty at King Cleaners have been able to do? Clearly, the trademark cannot explain the variability in survival rates or in profits since the trademark impacts each franchisee equally. Likewise, advertising, marketing, training, or other factors that may appear at first to account for differential success within franchise systems are also nonfactors since they are also applied to each franchisee equally. And although a poor location is often used as an excuse by underperforming franchisees, the empirical evidence points to operational factors as more critical than geographical factors. For instance, at King Cleaners franchisees are free to market their business in vast areas, and it is quite common to find high-performance and low-performance franchisees operating in the same location. And even when location is fixed, as it is at Sign Masters and Star Muffler, operational factors may be more critical to franchisee success. As Mark Spinelli from Star Muffler once remarked, "In our business we have found that operational factors account for franchisee success because we can sell an under-performing unit to a new guy, and the sales just take off. If it was a poor location, no one would be able to turn the sales around."

But which operational factors, which activities, are most critical to franchisee survival and profits, especially if franchisees are trained according to the franchisor standards? As Scott noted above, it is not only the day-to-day skills of running a business that impacts franchisee survival but also the ability of franchisees to exploit the network of relationships and form alliances with others. Naturally, of all the relationships that operate within franchising the most common one to investigate is the franchisor-franchisee relationship itself. Economists from the principal-agent perspective outlined in chapter 1 would start with a basic question: since franchisees are geographically dispersed and cannot be easily monitored, how can a franchisor ensure that they do not shirk or otherwise take excessive leisure? Stated in this way, it is clear that principal-agent economists are interested in understanding franchising from the franchisor's perspective. The central problem is one of control: how can the franchisor control the franchisee? The answer is that if the interests of franchisors and franchisees are tightly aligned—as they are if both parties share revenues—then each will be working toward a common goal, and the shirking and excessive leisure are less likely to occur. The royalty payment (based upon gross sales) serves to align parties, and both the franchisor and franchisees have incentives to increase performance through higher revenues.

Of course, the question could be reversed and one would have a very different focus: "How can franchisees (who are geographically dispersed and unable to monitor the franchisor) ensure that the franchisor does not shirk from its responsibilities and take excessive leisure?" To my knowledge this question of "reverse shirking" has not been posed by principal-agent economists, although it is theoretically very interesting. In fact, underlying principal-agent economics is a moral philosophy in which managers, or in this case, franchisors, are assumed to be superior to the people they manage—to be harder workers, more trustworthy, less likely to "shirk." With these assumptions, the question of reverse shirking would never materialize. Consequently, the view of franchising from the principal-agent perspective is one-sided, excessively narrow, and focused on how franchisors can control franchisees.

The view that franchise systems are arenas in which parties attempt to control each other is not limited to principal-agent economists, however. When I tell people in the franchise industry—executives, franchisees, lawyers, or consultants—that I conduct research on franchising I am invariably asked, "Whose side are you on, the franchisor side or the franchisee side?" This bifurcation of franchising into two neat and mutually exclusive categories makes franchising tractable, but unrealistic. The complexity of franchising extends far beyond the franchisor-franchisee relationship to include other obvious parties such as customers and suppliers, but also not-so-obvious parties such as relatives and friends. Indeed, the social capital within franchise systems extends to five basic relationships—franchisor-franchisee, franchisee-franchisee (peer-to-peer), franchisee-customer, franchisee-supplier, and what I term the "kinship network." Of these many relationships, the franchisor-franchisee, the peer-to-peer, and the kinship network relationships impact franchisee survival and profits.

THE FRANCHISOR-FRANCHISEE NETWORK

"Which do you think is a better model for managing a company," Mark Spinelli of Star Muffler once asked me, "the Old Testament or the New Testament?"

"I don't know," I replied in a surprised tone, "probably the New Testament."

"I used to think so, too, but now I think that the Old Testament is better. I think you can get in trouble managing from a New Testament perspective. Let me tell you what I mean. We have guys that take advantage of us, take advantage of our kindness, and they're really a cancer in the system. We find a guy who is not upholding our standards and we listen to his story, we try to help him out, we give him a second, third, or fourth chance. If anything, we're too understanding about it. But we're the ones that end up getting hurt because they take advantage of us. And it's not just us, they take advantage of their employees, of their customers, or their wife and kids—really, it's everybody they come into contact with. We find that these guys have a trail of deceit, of lies that they've been telling everybody. When we finally get them out of the system the other guys say, 'What took you so long?' because they know the guy's a cancer in the system."

"Well, how many cancer spots do you have?"

"Not very many. But it's human nature to want to be liked—we have that need just like everybody else, but it can be used against us. We have to keep the system pure, and now if we find a guy that doesn't hold our standards or a guy that is stealing from us we punish him, just like they would in the Old Testament."

"Is that the hard part?" I asked.

"Yeah, it is, but nobody ever said this was easy. We've had to let some guys go—they just would not follow the system—and it's been tough on everybody. But sometimes these guys come back and say, 'You know, you guys were the first ones to ever hold me accountable to something.' So in the end, it's gratifying to know that we helped someone along, even if it is in a totally unexpected way."

Mark was silent for a moment and then continued: "You see, not everyone is a good guy. We bring them in thinking that they are, but a lot of people are good at hiding their true nature. Over time, we figure out that they're really a cancer in the system."

"So what do you do differently now, anything?"

"Yeah. We make it much more difficult to buy one of our units. We have people waiting to buy a unit, but we won't sell them one if we're not confident that they'll be a good fit for our system. We have a controlled approach to growing the system—we don't want to grow too fast because we can't give the full value to the franchisees. We give a prospective franchisee a series of tasks and send him around to various franchisees and then get the feedback of all the franchisees. Usually sometime in the process a potential franchisee will let their true colors show. They won't do it in front of us but they'll think that the other franchisees will be impressed. So if we hear back from franchisees that they're concerned about something, then we just don't bring the guy in.

"The other thing we do is lead with a stronger hand. That's what the guys want. They don't want a participatory management structure. They want us to lead. So now we tell them, 'We lead and you follow.' "

"That's what they want?"

"Right. They want us to be vigilant about the purity of the system and to weed out those guys who are not upholding our standards."

For Spinelli and the Star Muffler executive team, the interactions with franchisees are influenced by their autocratic management style, a style that works given the particular environmental constraints the company faces. For instance, at Star Muffler the critical uncertainty facing a new franchisee is either converting an existing unit to the new format or building a new unit in a new location. Either way, the problems associated with start-up concern leasing arrangements with landlords, financing with banks or other financial institutions, or working with contractors, developers, or others involved in construction. Since most franchisees have little or no experience in real estate negotiations, build-outs, or financing, Star Muffler has the opportunity to build goodwill with franchisees and establish its authority by taking over these functions. Indeed, Star Muffler has much experience with the standard transactions involved in the opening of new units, and the company provides significant value to franchisees during the critical start-up phase. One consequence of providing a lot of value to new franchisees is that Star Muffler reaffirms its "We lead, you follow" strategy because the franchisee experience is one in which they are led through the maze of real estate, construction, and financing by Star Muffler management.

After this initial start-up phase, though, the autocratic interactions between Star Muffler and franchisees are more difficult to sustain because franchisees have a deep understanding of the undercar industry and a passion for cars. For instance, the training Star Muffler provides at the start-up stage is more like a refresher course in automotive services than it is an introduction for automotive neophytes because so many franchisees enter from within the industry. When I asked franchisees about start-up training, they often replied similar to one who stated, "I learned something about Star Muffler's approach to customers and sales, but not much about car repairs. I knew a lot about cars coming in to this." I once asked Spinelli why he recruited so many people from within the industry. He responded, "We'd really like to be able to sell a franchise unit to someone from outside the industry, to women and other people who don't have experience in the industry."

"Why don't you?" I asked.

"We just can't get them in here. We don't get any interest except from guys that like to work on their cars, and those are usually guys that are working as a manager in a dealership or in another franchise system. In fact, the other day we were talking about a franchisee we sold a unit to a couple of months ago. We thought he'd be good. He has a background in the industry and is well-educated. Well, he's starting out and needs some help so we sent a manager over to help and the guy has his wife there working the front desk, so we teach her the operations and Peter,

I have to tell you that she was fantastic. I mean, she was way better than anyone else in the system. She followed our process completely, she was honest with customers, treated them right, answered the phone in the correct way. We'd love to have a whole system filled with people like her, but we can't find them."

"What happened with her, did she stay working?"

"No, after Ken got the unit up and going she went back to doing whatever it was she did before. But the management team here wishes that we sold the franchise to her and not to him."

It is rare for Star Muffler to recruit people from outside the industry. Instead, most franchisees enter with specialized skills in car repair. This forces management to interact with franchisees with the "strong hand" that Spinelli spoke of because the company needs to break bad habits and retrain franchisees in Star Muffler methods. At King Cleaners and Sign Masters, quite often the opposite situation occurs. Since Sign Masters is in an emergent industry, none of the franchisees entered with specialized knowledge about sign making, and the value that Sign Masters provided franchisees at start-up was in learning this craft. The company could have provided more value by performing some of the real estate and financing functions necessary at start-up, but did not do so. Even so, once franchisees learned the craft, there was little in terms of value that Sign Masters could provide, and this impacted Beyer's ability to control the system. More important, it impacted the nature of interactions between the Sign Masters management team and franchisees: if there is little value to be added by the company, franchisees could easily dismiss the leadership role of management. In fact, Beyer admitted that the major issue he faced with franchisees was in marketing, not in the technical aspects of creating signs. In the technical areas, in products, and in sales, franchisees had greater knowledge about the business than the franchisor.

Finally, at King Cleaners there were no up-front negotiations with lenders, builders, or landlords because most franchisees started out as a home-based unit and then upgraded to an office if the circumstances warranted it. Like at Sign Masters, most franchisees were not experienced in the maintenance business or if they were (like Scott, who worked for a franchisee through college), they did not have experience marketing in the business-to-business environment. But unlike Sign Masters, which was quickly outpaced by its own franchisees in many areas, King Cleaners provided value to franchisees in marketing their services to large, complex companies. Although the King Cleaners trademark provided the necessary legitimacy and credibility to franchisees in their negotiations with sophisticated managers, many franchisees still lacked the self-confidence to speak with the facilities manager of a Fortune 500 company. The main task of master distributors John and Barbara was to help people overcome this mental barrier, which they did through ongoing monthly seminars. Also, it was not uncommon for John to accompany franchisees on sales calls if a potential client were particularly critical to the franchisee. Rusty, who didn't need any help selling, would convince John to visit potential clients with him nonetheless. "You cannot refuse King Cleaners if me and John are in the room making the presentation," Rusty once said to me. "The two of us, when we team up, are unstoppable. John's a great salesman, and it's a lot of fun to sell as a team."

This collaborative relationship between John and Rusty underscores the importance of social capital in franchising, and it is an effective strategy to manage what can be an unwieldy system. The natural condition of social capital within franchise systems—at least between the franchisor and franchisees—may be decay. Over time, the interactions between franchisor and franchisee can become predictable, less frequent, and less valuable. The source of decay stems in part from the natural progression of franchisees in gaining knowledge about their business. As franchisees grow in their knowledge about the local market, customers, and products, as well as in the business cycles that impact their sales, they come to know more about the business than does the franchisor. The franchisor role as font of knowledge, guiding hand, or mentor, diminishes. It is difficult to lead a company if the people you are leading know more than you, but it is even more challenging to be paid for your expertise if in fact you do not have any. While the conditions that give rise to social capital decay are endemic to franchising, the response by franchisors to offset that decay can vary widely.

Spinelli and Star Muffler preferred an authoritarian approach, John and Barbara from King Cleaners a collaborative approach, and Stu Beyer and the Sign Masters executive team, a laissez faire or avoidance approach. In the short run, during start-up, franchisors have an opportunity to capitalize on the asymmetry in knowledge about the business to establish strong levels of social capital, but in the long run they need to provide value on an on-going basis. The ability to add long-term value is compounded by the high turnover rates within each system. All three franchisors had a small number of people with long tenures and quite a bit of turmoil in the early stages of franchising. The continual stream of new franchisees, coupled with the immediacy of their needs in opening a new location, forced all three companies to exert more effort in developing relationships with early-stage franchisees and to neglect, somewhat, the needs of existing franchisees. The obvious impact of this situation is a decrease in social capital with existing and long-term franchisees, which impairs the franchisor's ability to achieve rapid change, hinders quick decisions, and slows the company's ability to implement new programs and procedures. The nonobvious impact that declining social capital has on the system is in the peer-to-peer relationships among franchisees.

COMRADES AND COMPETITORS

"Do you ever compete with anybody?" I asked Doug and George, the brother-in-laws from King Cleaners.

"We compete with everybody," said George.

"No, I mean with other franchisees in the system."

"Oh, I see. Well, we won't compete if it's a good person, and we won't compete if someone stays in their own territory," said George.

"But if someone comes into our territory," broke in Doug, "then we'll go after something in theirs."

"And," added George, "if they're not a good guy, we'll compete, too."

"Yeah, that's right," said Doug, "We'll go after accounts in another territory if we think a guy's not good."

"What do you mean by that? What's a good guy and a bad guy?"

"A good guy is someone who operates their business well, treats their customers and employees well, and stays in their territory," Doug replied. "A bad guy is a person who doesn't follow through, doesn't follow the King Cleaners approach."

"Or," said George, "we just don't like him."

"Are there a lot of those people here?"

"Well, you've seen 'em, haven't you? Not everyone is as talented as me and George," Doug said with a laugh.

"Yeah, but I don't want to make judgments about whether they're good guys or bad guys—"

"Well, you don't have to," replied Doug, "but we do. See, John will sell a franchise to anybody. As far as I know he's never refused anyone. If you've got the money and you want to come in, then the door's wide open. And you know, it doesn't take a whole lot of money to get in here, so there are a lot of people that King Cleaners lets in that shouldn't be here."

"So you compete against those guys?"

"Yep," said George.

"How do you feel about that?"

"About what?" George asked.

"About competing with other franchisees."

"About competing with other franchisees!" George exclaimed with a puzzled look, "I have no problem with it at all!"

"But don't you have enough competitors out there without competing against the King Cleaners franchisees?"

"I see where you're going with this," said Doug. "Yeah, there's a tension there, you know, he's my brother, but I compete against him, too. But that's just the way it is. We didn't choose to do it this way—we'd just as soon act like a solid force with all the franchisees on the same page, but people come in here and they think they own their own business, and they're going to do what they have to do, just like me and George."

Relationships among franchisees—the peer-to-peer network of social capital—are difficult to develop and sustain for a number of reasons. As George and Doug pointed out, there are inherent tensions within the franchisee-franchisee relationship, and there is a perception that others impact one's own survival and profitability. The other franchisees in the system are potential competitors operating under the same trademark, using roughly the same operating methods and marketing materials and pursuing similar customers. There is perhaps a natural tendency to avoid interacting with a competitor or to assume that a competitor would not want to interact with you. For instance, I once asked a franchisee at Star Muffler if he ever had a chance to visit Pete Morgan's operation and he replied, "Pete Morgan doesn't divulge anything to anyone. Successful people rarely give you any clues." But when I asked Pete Morgan about interacting with others in the system I received a different response.

"What do the other franchisees think of you, do you know?"

"Yeah, I think they feel like they can't talk to me."

"Why is that, do you suppose?"

"Well, I guess it's jealousy, I don't know."

"Suppose someone called you up for advice, would you help them out?"

"Yeah, sure. I don't see why I wouldn't help. It's not like they're going to take any business away from me. Look how close the next closest guy is to me—it's at least a twenty-minute drive away from here and in this business no customer is going to drive an extra twenty minutes. Besides, nearly all of my customers are repeat customers, and I get a lot of people through word of mouth. Anyway, I'd like to be a mentor to some of these young guys coming in, but I don't get approached."

"When I look at your facilities it seems that your shop is not as nice as some of the new units going up . . . "

"Oh yeah, I only have three bays and I still have a sign from before we switched to the new colors."

"And, you know, looking out at your waiting room and, well,

at the cars in the lot, it seems like you have a lot of lower income customers."

"Yeah, they're almost all lower income. Those are the only people that need to fix their cars. Rich people lease or trade in their cars so they never have to do the type of maintenance we do. We don't compete for rich people, and we don't get the do-it-yourselfer—but everyone else is a possible customer."

"But there's a perception among some of the franchisees that you're fixing mostly Lincolns and Cadillacs up here . . . "

"Just some of them?" he laughed "Yeah, I know they think I have a lot of big ticket items, but my business is no different from anyone else's."

"Does anyone ever come by to visit, any of the other franchisees?"

"No, not really."

"It seems like it would be good for them to see your operations, like it would change some of the myths out there."

"Yeah, I think it'd be good, but I don't see it happening."

"So do you even compete with any other franchisees?"

"Oh, on some level. I've been the highest revenue franchisee for pretty many years in a row now, and I want to continue that. That's the standard that we're measured by and I want to push myself to be the best. But if you mean, do I try to go out and get customers from another franchisee? No, I wouldn't ever do that. For one thing, I don't have to, and for another, that's not the way I operate my business."

George and Doug from King Cleaners compete with everyone, and Pete Morgan from Star Muffler competes with no one, but even so, franchisees know that others impact their business. As Pete Morgan stated, "We're all under the same trademark, like it or not." Yet franchisees do not choose their colleagues and they cannot control who enters the system. What if a "bad guy" is in the neighboring community; what recourse does a franchisee have? Not much, as it turns out, even though franchisors and franchisees agree that there are "bad guys" out there. As Spinelli of Star Muffler pointed out, neither franchisors nor franchisees can easily determine if someone is a "good guy" until after he has entered the system.

In addition to the threat of people within the same system operating outside of the trademark, that is, not operating their franchise according to franchise standards, franchisees are also impacted by the location of new units. But here, too, franchisees have little or no say about where new franchise units will be located, nor do they have much say in the growth schedule a franchisor will pursue. Although Spinelli at Star Muffler pursued a "controlled growth" plan of expansion, that's the rare exception: most franchisors wish instead to grow as rapidly as possible and saturate the market. Both Stu Beyer from Sign Masters and John from King Cleaners would sell as many units as they could find buyers. One franchisee from King Cleaners, when asked about quality standards among franchisees, stated, "I think John just lets the market take care of the bad ones." Today, territorial disputes between franchisees and franchisors are a major source of litigation as franchisees attempt to insulate themselves from others, and franchisors seek to penetrate the market. All of these factors significantly impact a franchisee's bottom line, and they impact the degree to which franchisees will interact with others in the system.

The third main factor that limits the development of social capital within franchisee networks is the entrepreneurial framework driving most people to enter franchise systems in the first place. Like most entrepreneurs, franchisees are likely to want to conduct their business on their own, be their own boss, and work independently. Consequently, they are less likely to seek advice from their peers. In addition to an individualistic orientation, franchisees also have to overcome logistical factors in order to develop high levels of social capital. One franchisee commented, "When you work sixty hours a week, it's hard to find the time to talk to all these people." And the geographical dispersion of franchisees further limits face-to-face interaction. Although King Cleaners, Sign Masters, and Star Muffler each held an annual meeting, the meeting was not so much a time to interact with others as it was a time for the franchisor to discuss the year's accomplishments and introduce the upcoming marketing campaign. Both King Cleaners and Star Muffler had monthly meetings, but for Star Muffler the meetings were only open to the franchisor executive team and the franchisee advisory council—a franchisor-appointed board of six franchisees.

The final factor that discourages the formation of social ties with other franchisees is the general turnover within each system. With relatively high turnover rates, existing franchisees—those that survive—are much further along the learning curve and have fewer instrumental reasons to interact with newcomers. Established franchisees have repeat business, a strong customer base, and know the business inside and out. In fact, there are very few situations that would arise in any franchise system that would require an existing franchisee to seek the help and advice of a newcomer. So most interactions between start-up franchisees and existing franchisees are one-sided, with new franchisees seeking advice and help from existing franchisees. It is not the case that existing franchisees do not provide advice, as Pete Morgan of Star Muffler mentioned, but more the case that the need to interact with others is quite low.

Given all of these factors—the natural tendency to view others as competitors, an entrepreneurial ideology that insists on individualism over collaboration, logistical obstacles such as time and distance, and a knowledge system that is oriented toward nonreciprocity, it is not surprising that connections among franchisees are difficult to establish, infrequent, and temporary. Yet social capital plays a crucial role in franchisee survival, as Scott pointed out earlier, and in franchisee performance. In fact, of all the factors considered—such as age, experience, career path, location—none are more important in explaining franchisee performance than social capital. In all three companies, franchisees with the highest sales were not only most active in establishing connections with others but also were most frequently the recipients of others' connections. Those with high sales were the most highly trusted, had many friendships throughout the system, and were well-respected, while those with low sales tended to be less active in establishing a peer-to-peer network and were more likely to be isolated.

Within the franchisee network the ability to get along with others is critical to franchisee success. I asked franchisees, "Which people do you find it most uncomfortable to be around or to associate with? Whom do you find it difficult or awkward to be around or deal with?" Predictably, people who were considered "awkward" or uncomfortable to deal with were less likely to have many friends, were not trusted, and were not as respected as others. They also had lower sales. But surprisingly, these awkward people were more likely to be in close proximity to others, which is at first rather puzzling. Regardless of where franchisees are located, their closest neighbors are the most awkward people they have to deal with. Why is it not the case that particular persons are awkward, rather than those who are closest? Of course, there were people within each franchise who receive more than their fair share of nominations for being awkward, and Scott from King Cleaners even commented, "[M]ost people probably think I'm awkward to deal with"—and as it turns out, he was correct. But the more important result is that awkwardness is directly proportional to close proximity.

One explanation for the relationship between awkwardness and proximity might be that franchisees have no control over who enters the system or the location of new units. Although these decisions are wholly determined by the franchisor, there are externalities associated with the actions of one's neighbors. These externalities have an even greater impact because franchisees face a limited market that they share with other service providers who are nearly perfect substitutes. Any harm or damage that accrues to the franchise system because of one's neighbors is a damage that has to be absorbed by franchisees because they are not free to pick up and relocate their units to a new area. While the costs of harm to the company's trademark are borne by all franchisees, it is those who are closest to the offender that bear the greater cost. The relationship between awkwardness and close proximity defines the tension within the peer-to-peer relationship since the potential for gain and the potential for disaster increase as the company sells new franchise units to penetrate and saturate markets.

While proximity and awkwardness is one dynamic within the franchisee network, proximity has another unanticipated consequence: In all three companies, people in closest proximity to others have the highest sales. That is, it appears that there are gains for franchisees who are surrounded by others, and it is, therefore, because of competition with others, rather than in spite of it, that these franchisees excel. Perhaps people who operate their franchise in densely occupied markets capitalize on the presence of others by exploiting the mistakes and weaknesses of other franchisees. Perhaps there are increasing returns once a critical mass in franchise units is achieved. Or perhaps as franchisees find themselves competing against others operating under the same trademark, the response that leads to higher performance is the one in which the quality of service delivered to the customer is increased. Nevertheless, franchisees who seek to distance themselves from others in order to escape competition and capture a monopoly in their own local markets may be disappointed in the results because it is competition with perfect substitutes, rather than isolation from them, that leads to higher performance.

Survival and success within franchising are difficult to achieve, yet there are people like Rusty from King Cleaners and Pete Morgan from Star Muffler that not only survive, but prosper. Although Rusty and Pete differ in a number of personal characteristics, they share a common profile in terms of their social capital—both are active in terms of seeking and receiving connections with others. It is not necessarily the level of connectedness that is so critical, for nearly everybody in a franchise system has contact with others. Rather, the critical factor is the diversity of ties to others. For instance, at King Cleaners and Sign Masters there were strong cliques of female networks—dense, frequent, and strong ties among the women in the franchise. In King Cleaner's case the network centered around Barbara, the wife of John. At Sign Masters, there were strong ties among all female franchisees and a strong tie to the vice president of marketing, Michelle. But Rusty was also strongly connected to the women's network at King Cleaners; similarly, Victor, a high-performance franchisee at Sign Masters, was also strongly connected to the women's network.

The profile of a successful franchisee involves high degrees of social capital—an external focus on interactions with many others in the system. This is a challenging strategy for many franchisees to pursue, however. It not only goes counter to the entrepreneurial ideology surrounding franchising, but it also takes a lot of energy from people who are working long hours to begin with. In addition, since franchisees compete with others either directly or indirectly (for prestige and status), there is a natural tendency to avoid interacting with some others in the system. But it is telling that the people who are least likely to need to interact with others—the successful franchisees who have established customers, predictable revenue streams, and great knowledge about the business—are the ones with high social capital.

### KINSHIP NETWORK

A final form of social capital that is prevalent and important within franchise systems is the kinship network. The defining element, the common characteristic endemic to nearly all franchise systems, perhaps, is that franchisees rely on relatives for help, advice, support, capital, expertise, and labor. Without the strong kinship network, survival is difficult, as Scott from King Cleaners pointed out. "You can't make it on your own. Look at everyone else in the system—no one is single like me. They all have, you know, a wife or husband who helps out, and Dan, he's got his dad working in the back fixing broken equipment. Me? I'm all by myself, and you just can't do it." Scott, of course, joined an alliance with Dan and Chuck, two franchisees who had overlapping territories. But for many franchisees, survival depends on social capital with family members. In some instances it's obvious that franchisees have strong kinship networks, like George and Doug, the brothers-in-law from King Cleaners, or Victor and Marge from Sign Masters. Yet in other instances it is not obvious that the franchise unit is operated as a family business until the status quo is upset—perhaps through a divorce or death. CEO of Star Muffler Mark Spinelli learned that the driving force behind one franchisee's success was his wife who, unfortunately, only worked in the unit temporarily.

At King Cleaners, Sign Masters, and Star Muffler the percentage of franchisees who worked with family members was very high—exceeding 75 percent, and franchisees who operated alone, like Scott, were the exception. Even people like Pete Morgan from Star Muffler and Rusty from King Cleaners relied on help from their extended kinship network. In Rusty's case, his sister worked in the front office. In Pete Morgan's case, his father had helped him in the start-up stage of his business. By the time I worked with Pete, he had been operating for well over ten years and his father was no longer involved, but at the start his involvement was critical. "I didn't have any money when I started out and I was pretty young. The company at the time really didn't offer any support, and I realized that I was going to have to learn this by myself. My dad helped out a lot when I first started. He countersigned on a loan and together we figured out how to run the business."

The kinship network that franchisees exploited was not limited just to their spouse, but extended to sons and daughters, brothers and sisters, cousins and nephews, fathers and mothers. The high incidence of family members in franchising suggests that franchise companies have institutionalized and reincarnated the mom-and-pop retail enterprise so prevalent at the turn of the century. But unlike that earlier form and in contrast to today's mom-and-pop franchisees, many franchisees who relied upon the assistance of family members were sophisticated and had extensive capital reserves. The term "mom-and-pop" is a negative one within franchising, but neo-franchisees like Pete Morgan and Rusty were just as likely to employ family members as disillusioned franchisees and sideliners. In fact, nearly all franchisees, because of the risks they faced, the amount of work required, and the operation's need for direct oversight, depended upon family members, a trusted and reliable source of labor, advice, expertise, and capital.

The dense and extensive kinship networks that characterize franchising can lead to severe management problems for franchisors, problems often not encountered by executives and managers within other corporate forms. Franchise companies have, perhaps unwittingly, retained one of the oldest organizational forms in existence, the family enterprise. The juxtaposition of a traditional form of organization like the family business or cottage industry with a "new" strategy like franchising only appears idiosyncratic because we naturally assume that organizational forms evolve to more complex structures over time. But as Abbott argues, labor mechanisms based upon tradition are "easily overlooked in modern society."[1]

1. Andrew Abbott, "The New Occupational Structure: What Are the Questions?" *Work and Occupations* 6 (August 1989): 279.

# CHAPTER 8

FRANCHISOR UNCERTAINTIES

Not long ago, a regional trade association of franchisors asked if I could make a presentation at one of their meetings.

"What would be a good topic?" I asked

"Do you know anything about finding high-quality franchisees? We could really use a program that tells us what types of people are good franchisees. How do we go after these people? Where do we find them?"

The concern about recruiting high-quality franchisees was warranted because the "input" of franchisees, a key uncertainty facing franchisors, proved to be a Herculean task. Stu Beyer of Sign Masters was desperate as he stated, with no small measure of anxiety, "I've had a helluva time getting good prospects." But unlike other organizations that merely sell products, franchise companies have to sell a product—the franchise unit—as well as a philosophy, a method of conduct, and an operating procedure.

Consequently, how these companies went about selling a franchise—the message they promoted and the tone they set—had tremendous consequences for how easy it would be to manage franchisees later on. As Beyer noted, "We offer three weeks of training, and that's more than others in the industry. I tell you, though, the start has everything to do with how things go later."

The task was even more difficult for Spinelli at Star Muffler. "We only recruit on values. We bring a guy in and we spend most of our time figuring out what his values are, if they are close to our values. We try to determine if he will be the type of person that will work hard, put the customer first, and do what's right for the good of the chain. We don't want any lone operators, and we don't care if a guy doesn't have any money. In fact, the other day I was at a restaurant, and our waiter was fantastic. He had all the qualities we look for in a franchisee, so we struck up a conversation. I asked him if he ever thought about operating his own business. Well, he did, and we went through several intense days of interviewing."

"What happened with that prospect?" I asked.

"I thought we had him, and we would have but his wife was against the idea of owning a franchise. And that's good to find out beforehand because if your family is not behind you, you'll probably fail. But I want to say, this guy didn't know anything about the car business, and he didn't have much money. Those two things we can solve. It's our business to train a guy in the proper methods in how to run our shops, and we can always get financing. We can even do it ourselves if we have to. But it is far more difficult to find someone who shares our values."

Recruiting was one of two major uncertainties that franchisors faced. The other was managing franchisees once they recruited them. These were interrelated since franchisee expectations were often set during the initial conversations and visits, and expectations were reinforced by the brochures and materials provided to them during their recruitment. One such expectation, quite commonly put forth by franchisors in their recruiting efforts, was that franchise ownership was equivalent to entrepreneurship. In fact, nearly every advertisement involving franchise opportunities embraced the ideology of entrepreneurship. In the *Franchise Opportunities Guide,* a publication by the preeminent trade group for the industry, the International Franchise Association, advertisements consistently espoused and promoted the ideology of entrepreneurship:

> "For the price of a new car you can drive your own business."
> "You will be in business for yourself . . . but not by yourself."
> "Discover your power potential. Join the fast growing list of

entrepreneurs who have secured their futures with (Company X) franchise."

"The key to a successful business of your own . . . could be (this) franchise."

"Stop making money for someone else. Take control of your future as the owner of your own franchise."[1]

The advertisements all promote the idea of "owning a business" and that by owning a business one is an "entrepreneur." Of course, it is not unreasonable to equate business ownership with entrepreneurship; indeed, in research literature on entrepreneurship there exist two definitions of "entrepreneur."[2] One definition is of the "firm-organizing" person; the other definition is that of the person who "creates" something new or different. But in equating franchise ownership with entrepreneurship franchisors have inadvertently complicated management of franchisees.

"Selling franchising as 'owning your own business' was a huge mistake," said Mark Spinelli of Star Muffler. "It was the wrong approach, and it's killing us as an industry. We constantly run into the problem of guys saying, 'I own it,' or 'I bought this franchise, and you can't tell me what to do.' And we don't want to use the contract to keep these guys in line. We can—we have the power to do that—but it's better to keep people motivated and aligned to a common purpose."

"Well," I asked, "what did they buy?"

"They only bought the right to operate our stores under the trademark. That's it. We own the trademark, and their only responsibility is to us, to follow our system and methods. What we do now is, we tell a guy, 'Look, we have a system, and we know it works. Your job is to come in to a store and follow that

1. International Franchise Association, *Franchise Opportunities Guide* (Washington, D.C.: International Franchise Association, 2000).

2. For a classic introduction to entrepreneurship, see Joseph Schumpeter's The Theory of Economic Development, 2d ed. (Cambridge: Harvard University Press). For a more recent discussion of research on entrepreneurship, see William J. Baumol, "Formal Entrepreneurship Theory in Economics: Existence and Bounds," *Journal of Business Venturing* 8 (1993): 197–210.

system. Now, we can't promise that you'll be a millionaire, but if you follow the system you'll make money.' And that's it. No more of this 'owning your own business' or 'be your own boss.' What we've come to realize is that these guys aren't entrepreneurs; they might think that they're entrepreneurs, but they're not. If they were really entrepreneurs, they'd go out and start their own business. More importantly, we don't want entrepreneurs; we're looking for people that share our values and will operate according to our standards. We need people who will follow our system. Whether the guy becomes wealthy is not important. That's what we sell now. It's not 'own your own business,' but 'operate one of our businesses according to our values and standards.' "

"Does anyone really want to put up the capital necessary to buy a unit just so they can operate it as a manager?"

"Sure. We have a queue of guys waiting to buy a unit. But even though we're looking for operators rather than entrepreneurs, they're not the same as managers. None of our managers make nearly as much as franchisees, and we also do not let managers operate more than one unit. For franchisees, we encourage them to expand and own multiple units, in part because they can make more money, but also if they are good managers they provide opportunities for other guys in their business to grow and develop. We want to expand our system, and if we can do that internally with our current franchisees, then that's better for us and them."

Unfortunately, not everyone was as enlightened as Mark Spinelli. Most participants—franchisors and franchisees alike—believed that franchising was a form of entrepreneurship. Franchisees commonly believed themselves to be entrepreneurs, to be in control of their business, to be solely responsible for the business decisions. Since most franchisees depleted most, if not all, of their personal fortunes purchasing a franchise, they were likely to respond as one did, "We take all the risk." So, after franchisees are recruited into franchising as entrepreneurs, their risk-taking perpetuates this belief. Even if franchisors were to abstain completely from an entrepreneurial metaphor in promoting franchising, the belief by franchisees that they are truly entrepreneurs would be difficult to eradicate precisely because many believed business ownership equaled entrepreneurship.

For many people, this is the "American Dream," and it is what defines a person as successful—to be independent, to be one's own boss, to own something. Like it or not, franchisors must manage people who subscribed to this worldview. But franchisees' entrepreneurial self-perceptions undermine franchising for it promotes a spirit of independence that runs counter to the collectivist underpinnings demanded by a successful franchise system.

As Spinelli pointed out earlier, when faced with a disagreement on any particular issue with a franchisor, franchisees were likely to invoke an "I own this business" argument, and franchisors to quickly counter with "No, you don't. It's our trademark." By believing that they were entrepreneurs, franchisees experienced tension between the independence, autonomy, and self-direction they believed were rightfully theirs with the control, surveillance, and dependency that they experienced. The dissonance that results can be traced back to something as fundamental as the very definition of "franchisee," and it caused tensions in the system and led to misalignment among franchisors and franchisees.

While shrouding franchising under the veil of entrepreneurship was an obvious mistake franchisors committed while recruiting franchisees, other elements of recruiting that impacted franchisors were not nearly so obvious. Two clearly important factors—over which franchisors had little or no control—were the motives for people to buy a franchise unit and the careers they had prior to becoming a franchisee. It may seem that motives for franchisees to buy a franchise would not be relevant for understanding franchise systems; after all, why someone decides to do something may have little impact on their later actions.

But that argument fails on two grounds. First, the growth of the franchise industry occurs either because more companies pursue the strategy or because the existing franchise companies expand. Either way, growth occurs if people are willing to buy a franchise unit or if existing franchisees are willing to purchase additional units. Since franchise demand is the engine, we might fruitfully ask why people are willing to put their life savings into a franchise system. Second, the motive for people to buy a franchise impacts their expectations of themselves and the franchisor both in the initial start-up phase of operating their business and in the long-term. What franchisees expect makes managing them either simple or extremely difficult for franchisors. I should note as an aside that the motives for firms to pursue franchising are straightforward, including expansion with someone else's capital, shifting of risk associated with a poor location away from the company, moving responsibility for an unreliable labor force to others, and smoothing market turbulence at the retail unit level.

But the motives of franchisees are not nearly as clear. In working with franchisees one of the first questions I immediately asked was, "Why did you buy a franchise?" I naively assumed that most people would respond as Rusty from King Cleaners did—that they wanted to make a lot of money, that franchising was an excellent investment opportunity. To be sure, several other franchisees did indicate financial returns as a motivating factor. "I was in business for myself, and I thought I could make more money with a franchise," stated one. If only it were the case that all prospective franchisees were motivated by financial returns, managing a franchise system would be simplified. Alas, no such alignment of motives existed, and instead franchisees indicated all sorts of reasons for buying a franchise unit. For some people, franchising allowed them to fulfill the "American Dream" of owning a business:

"I wanted the experience of owning my own business."

"I wanted to own my own business, and the values of King Cleaners fit my values."

"Ever since I was a little girl, I've always wanted to own my own business. Instead of fumbling by myself, I get guidance and help."

For others, franchising was a way to lessen the risk of starting something from scratch, either because of the leverage of the brand, size of the chain, company support, or higher success rate of franchising:

"I needed the prominence of the name."

"I wanted to get into a business that had an established name and reputation."

"I needed the know-how of the system."

"Basically, it was insecurity. I wanted moral and other support."

"I thought it would accelerate the speed of entry into the market."

"The percent failed is way higher for independent; we're led to believe that a franchise is safer."

"The statistics about making it, the security."

However, a large percentage of franchisees indicated that they had fewer career opportunities:

"I was desperate for a job. Both my husband and I were artists, and we had been unemployed and had no hope of finding anything."

"I had a golden parachute, and I needed to do something with it but I didn't want to work for anyone."

"I was a victim of a corporate acquisition, so I had a golden parachute."

"It was a case of necessity. The corporation I worked for disbanded and gave the option of buying a franchise."

"I lost my job after twenty years when I was fifty-five years old. What the hell else am I going to do? No one is going to hire someone my age."

And, finally, some franchisees were recruited into franchising:

"I worked for the company during school, and when I finished they asked me to buy."

"I was working menial jobs with no real potential or growth, and a guy at my church was an executive with King Cleaners. He encouraged me to buy a franchise."

One immediate problem with which franchisors must grapple is how to manage franchisees with wildly different motives. Some, like Rusty from King Cleaners, viewed their entry as an investment and demanded attention, while others wanted to be left alone. Some franchisees wanted to be their own boss and be independent, while others needed the support and help of the franchisor. The key point is not necessarily that everyone who buys a franchise wants to be an entrepreneur, but rather, the diversity of motives reflects the numerous expectations held by franchisees. Consequently, the ability of franchisors to adequately manage those divergent expectations is strained. Even if franchisors knew all of the expectations of franchisees, it is highly unlikely that they would be able to manage the system for so many different goals, preferences, and needs. Thus, franchisor uncertainties stemmed not only from the message they used to recruit people, but also from the preconceived notions franchisees had about franchising. More important, franchisor uncertainties were the result of elements completely out of their control, such as the motives and wants of franchisees. Again, the mindsets of franchisors and franchisees were misaligned because of these differing expectations.

In addition to preconceived notions about franchising, franchisors have no control over another important factor: the careers that precede franchising. Franchisors normally recruited people who had prior experience in various careers, and few—if any—franchisees graduated directly from high school and purchased a franchise unit. Although several franchisees graduated from college and immediately purchased a franchise, this route into franchising was extremely rare. Less than 1 percent of all franchisees entered with no prior work experience. Instead, franchisees entered franchising from a particular location in an occupational and institutional structure, and franchising represented a step on their career path. Because career paths are highly individualized, franchisees had different experiences and oftentimes, different expectations about "how things should be done." These differing expectations caused considerable managerial problems for franchisors but, surprisingly, were mostly an unrecognized source of uncertainty.

CAREER PATHS

There are three basic routes into franchising—vertical, horizontal, and random—and each impacts franchisors in significant ways. A vertical career move into franchising occurs when people in the franchisor corporate offices or employees of existing franchisees buy a franchise. It was fairly commonplace that employees were recruited by franchisees that wanted to escape the franchise system or by corporate sales representatives who found a good fit between an employee and the company. One franchisee offered this explanation of why he purchased a unit from his boss, "I thought I could do it. I saw the former owner do it, and I was working for him."

Others, like Tom at King Cleaners, were convinced by members of the corporate offices to purchase a franchise and were offered a "good deal" to buy the unit. Similar to Tom, many franchisees who bought a unit at the behest of the company purchased one in a small or rural market or in some other less-than-desirable location. Whenever possible, franchisors preferred to sell units to existing franchisees, to someone from the company with whom they were acquainted or, more important, to someone who knew the business.

"One of the benefits of selling to someone you know," stated Stu Beyer, "is that you know their capabilities. But if things don't work out it's much harder to deal with, since you destroy a relationship."

Spinelli from Star Muffler noted, "The sale goes through quicker if we sell to someone we know, but it is sometimes more difficult to manage. Other franchisees think that there is favoritism, and to tell you the truth, some of the people that we bring in who we know also expect special treatment. But we don't do that. We treat everybody the same."

Vertical career moves were more common at King Cleaners. Recruiting franchisees was difficult because the building maintenance industry was not exciting or interesting to outsiders, so people within King Cleaners were encouraged to purchase a unit. Having an intimate knowledge of people, understanding their capabilities, and knowing their values was of greater importance at King Cleaners because of the nature of the work carried out. Since franchisees provided cleaning services "on location," it was difficult for a franchisor to conduct a spot check on franchisees. It was pointless to call to find out if they were conducting the work and because the business did not require much inventory, a check of inventory levels provided little corroborating information about sales volume. At King Cleaners, the values of the potential franchisee and vertical career moves, where franchisees are known to the company beforehand, were most important.

A second type of career move, the horizontal career move, occurs when franchisees either enter from a different franchise system, so they know something about franchising, or they enter franchising from within the same industry, so they know something about the dynamics of the industry. Horizontal career paths were common at Star Muffler, and many franchisees not only had extensive knowledge about the industry prior to entering but they defined themselves as "car guys."

As one franchisee stated, "The reason I got into this business is because I like cars, but now I don't have any time to work on them. I only get one day off, and I can't even take the time to work on my own car." While it would seem that franchisors would prefer to recruit franchisees with extensive experience in the industry since the learning curve would be less steep, there was at least one major drawback for franchise companies: importing negative or inappropriate alternative practices. For instance, one franchisee who had previously worked at a car dealership service center gave advice to a nearby franchisee about how to price services: "I was taught to charge twenty dollars over list price for parts, but people don't want to pay for that and they'll shop around. They'll ask you, 'Why are your parts eighty-eight dollars when everyone else is selling them for sixty-eight dollars?' So, I add the twenty bucks in the labor because people don't question labor."

This practice, squeezing customers on labor charges, was exactly the type of pricing that Spinelli wished to obliterate from Star Muffler. But as he drove the company toward a customer-friendly and honest approach, franchisees with horizontal career paths jeopardized the entire system, complicating his quest increasingly. Horizontal entry into franchising, seemingly a good recruitment strategy, could be risky. Although the upside of lower training costs, greater knowledge base, and better understanding of the business moves these franchisees farther along the learning curve, the downside of importing nonfranchisor practices often outweighs these benefits.

A third career move into franchising involves what I term "random moves." In some respects, it is a residual category, for if franchisees have neither vertical nor horizontal career paths they would by default have a random one. Nevertheless, the random career path has important consequences for franchisors. In random moves, franchisees have little practical business experience and no real knowledge of the industry in which they are entering.

At Sign Masters, random career paths were the signature entry pattern of franchisees. More than 80 percent of the franchisees at Sign Masters first heard about the company at a franchise expo. Random entry into franchising may indicate a lack of job opportunities, or it may indicate people making a jump into a totally new career. Either way, franchisees that entered into a franchise system without any prior ideas or knowledge about franchising were often disappointed with the concept since the reality of franchising differed drastically from what they expected.

I posed this question to a franchisee at Star Muffler: "If you had to do it all over again, would you buy a franchise again?"

"That's kind of a Catch-22 question," he responded. "If I knew what I know now, I probably wouldn't, but you can't know what it's like until after you're in it."

Regardless of the career pattern of franchisees, there was an asymmetry in information and knowledge, with franchisors having the advantage over franchisees. Not only did the franchisor know how franchise systems should (or could) operate, but they knew the particular nuances of the industry, including the suppliers, customers, competitors, and the cycles of the market. They knew why franchisees were likely to fail and could discern from a balance sheet not only whether franchisees hit their targets but also how long a franchisee could stay at a particular level and still remain viable. The asymmetry in information was well known to franchisors. As Mark Spinelli of Star Muffler said, "We have an information advantage over any potential franchisee. We know the business better than he'll ever know, and we know more about him than he does about us."

## ALIGNMENT

Vertical, horizontal, and random patterns of entry present management problems for franchisors. Like the ideology of entrepreneurship used so often in recruiting franchisees, career patterns help explain differences in perspective and expectations between franchisors and franchisees. These differences can and do lead to problems of alignment. By alignment, I mean the extent to which franchisees and franchisors share the same interests in a broad sense, and more specifically, the extent to which franchisees and franchisors perceive that their goals and means to achieve them are congruent. The way franchisees are recruited into franchising, their motives for buying, and the careers that lead them to franchising all serve to misalign franchisees and franchisors, creating management headaches. Bill Parker of King Cleaners believed that the interests of the company and franchisees diverged and especially that franchisees wanted to (and did) operate their franchise in ways detrimental to the trademark. This belief was also widespread at other companies and at all management levels. It also was commonplace for franchisors to bemoan the lack of franchisee alignment with corporate goals and objectives.

A franchisor at Sign Masters stated, "Our interests differ slightly, mainly at how we approach customers. We want to increase sales, to expand sales, to have franchisees offer and sell more services. We think that by doing so, they'll increase their profits. But they want to increase profits not by increasing sales, but by streamlining." Another franchisor stated, "Their focus is too short-term and ours is long-term . . . their focus is at more of a finite or local level. Our focus is global—well, not global, but more of a national level." Still another franchisor said, "We want more money, but they want security more than money." So, to read between the lines, franchisees are frugal, parochial, narrow, and risk-averse. Stu Beyer from Sign Masters stated in frustration, "I'm beginning to realize that our interests differ—a lot. Too many franchisees don't want to grow, they're afraid to grow. They perceive that they can't get the work done if they grow too much, and so they stay within a limited range. Honestly! Sometimes I wonder why some of these people are even in business!"

Similarly, many franchisees believed that their interests differed from franchisors, that growth was not always to their benefit. One franchisee at Sign Masters stated, "It is not true in this situation that our interests are the same. I want more profitable sales, and the franchisor wants volume. The franchisor is also interested in selling additional franchise units and has interests in running corporate stores. Those latter two goals are not in my interests and may be counter to them if it takes their energy away from helping me." Another franchisee stated, "I want efficiency. Bigger numbers don't do anything for me if I can't keep the money." Yet another observed, "Our interests differ. They want growth, but they don't have to worry about operational factors. Growth can lead to more problems, for example, with finding high-quality employees."

A franchisee from Star Muffler stated, "The franchisor wants higher sales, and I want higher profits, but I have to be in the trenches with customers. There's only so much I can do to increase sales, while the franchisor has other ways to do it. It can open more units—and even use our advertising dollars to do it in the yellow pages, on billboards, and on TV to promote franchise opportunities. The franchisor has an advantage." Still another franchisee commented, "I don't know why and how they'd differ, but they differ in when a customer has a complaint. They tell us to do whatever it takes to keep the customer happy. Well, the money comes out of my pocket. They're not giving away their money."

Obviously, franchisees and franchisors have different end goals. Franchisees wish to maximize profits, and franchisors, maximize sales volume. While seemingly minor, the difference in end goal is in fact significant and impacts all aspects of operations, past, present, and future. But there are also differences in means or, more precisely, in the responsibilities, roles, and obligations for both parties. For franchisees, the obligations are very explicit and are articulated in the contract, reinforced during their initial training sessions and measured by franchisors throughout a franchisee's tenure.

Franchisees are evaluated during spot visits and phone calls, through customer satisfaction surveys, through an accounting of warranty repairs, and are constantly evaluated according to the actual sales levels and growth. Franchisors not only know the sales levels of each franchisee, but they can make valid comparisons to franchisees with similar market demographics and others who started at the same time, or using other characteristics instead. On the other hand, franchisors do not have an explicit set of expectations for themselves specified in the contract, and they are not subject to the same types of checks on their behavior. Franchisor expectations are not only subjective but are also elusive and fleeting.

A franchisee from Sign Masters stated, "Their product is more intangible, like moral support and training, management techniques, or even advice. I don't know how you can evaluate their end of the bargain."

Franchisees even had difficulty evaluating the "product" they purchased when they entered a franchise system. A King Cleaners franchisee stated, "All they sell you is paper—you know, goodwill, a good name, a reputation. All those things a banker wouldn't give you anything for."

Both the "product" and "support" franchisees received from franchisors were subjective and qualitative in nature and hindered their ability to evaluate the effectiveness of franchisors in delivering either one.

One cause for the misalignment in goals and means was the very different experience that franchisees and franchisors had within the same system. A common complaint from franchisees was that franchisors did not understand the business. "They don't know who our customers are," stated one franchisee. Another at Sign Masters stated, "They have this idea that our customer is a corporation that doesn't care about price, that just wants the product done quickly and reliably. I'd say that 10 percent of our customers are this way. Ninety percent are price-sensitive, small business people like us struggling to make it."

Another franchisee from King Cleaners echoed similar thoughts: "They don't know who my customers are. They don't know the local market."

Doug, a successful franchisee from King Cleaners who was a former executive at an international corporation, expanded on the problem of franchisors not knowing their customers. "Corporate does not understand that the fees we pay go directly to them," he stated. "They'll talk about being in a 'partnership' with franchisees, but that's not true. We're not partners, we're the best customers they'll ever have. Now, they don't treat us like customers, but that's what we are. We recruit for them, we train for them, we test new products, we buy all of our products and equipment from them, we go into clients that the corporate guys screw up or can't do. We're a captive market, but they sure don't treat us like valued customers. I'll give you an example. Remember the convention last year? Well, we paid for that—the franchisees. Ninety percent of the speakers were from the division—people who should be there anyway! But they didn't pay their own way there. The CEO told us that if we double our customer base in five years we'll have the next convention in Hawaii, and the franchisees gave him a standing ovation. I couldn't believe it! Of course, Corporate would want to go to Hawaii, but we'll have to pay to go there. The corporate guys will go for free. That's what I mean. We pay their salary, and we're the best customers they'll ever have."

Doug's insight, that franchisees *are* the customers, was an extremely perceptive understanding of the franchisee-franchisor relationship, but it did not go far enough. Franchisees not only paid income to the franchisor, they were a captive market. But most franchisors are not likely to support the notion of a captive market.

Although franchisees and franchisors understood that their end goal and means to achieve it differed, there were additional issues of alignment that were less transparent but that had consequences that were no less real. One particular issue—largely lost upon both franchisors and franchisees—was that many franchisees operated with a silent partner, notably a spouse. Spinelli from Star Muffler pointed out earlier that a spouse's approval of the purchase sometimes held up the sale of franchises, but the influence of the spouse extended far beyond this decision. Many franchisees (more than 75 percent) operated their business with the help of family members. Yet in all my discussions with franchisors and in all the meetings I attended, spouses and other family members were not present, and their needs, wants, desires, and perspective were neither solicited nor addressed.

Had those concerns been solicited franchisors might have learned something of value, for the spouses often had a detachment from the personalities of the franchise system that allowed them to be astute observers of the system. For instance, Barbara, the wife of John at King Cleaners, was more sought after than John for advice and she was more trusted by others, yet her opinions of management at King Cleaners were negative. "King Cleaners is not investing enough in the franchise end of the business," she once told me. "If you look at the annual report, all of our money goes to Corporate, but none of it comes back to us. Even the 800 number they established works against us because they receive the calls from customers, and they can send those customers out to anyone they want. I just don't think Corporate understands how important we are to the overall corporation."

Although seemingly innocuous as far as comments and opinions go, Barbara's special role in the franchise system gave her influence over other franchisees, especially women. Franchisors manage as if a lone individual owns/operates a franchise unit, but franchisees are dependent upon family members for labor and emotional support. Unlike other organizations, franchisors have to manage the silent partner to effectively control the franchise system.

Although recruiting high-quality franchisees was a concern shared by many franchisors, the uncertainties plaguing King Cleaners, Sign Masters, and Star Muffler extended far beyond this issue. Other factors, such as career paths, influenced the expectations of franchisees, impacted the actions they carried out, and contributed to misalignment between franchisees and franchisors. Franchise systems are very difficult organizations to manage with extreme uncertainty impacting all parts of the operation. From a certain perspective, it seems that there might not be any benefits to the strategy of franchising.

"What is the benefit of franchising?" I asked Mark Spinelli.

"The same as any other successful business—creating value."

But Stu Beyer, usually quite optimistic in his outlook said, "Some days—none."

"Really?" I asked. "I thought you liked franchising."

"Oh, I suppose a benefit is that you have the ability to expand and grow through others, and franchisees are more motivated than others, but there are a lot of drawbacks, too."

"What are those?" I asked.

"Well, you can have unreasonable franchisees, and then you're stuck with them. The problem is not that you don't have a contract to control them—you do—but it takes too long to get rid of them. They'll drag you through the courts, it'll take

a long time, and they'll be damaging the system with their negative attitude during the process. In a small system like ours, we
don't have the capital to fight franchisees in the courts. We don't
want to, we want to spend our money building the system. The
biggest complaint by franchisees is probably marketing, but if I
have to take a guy to court I can't spend the money in a way that
is for the good of the system. The other drawback is that you've
got independent-minded people, and it is difficult to keep the
system pure."

And a franchise manager from King Cleaners stated, "A major drawback is that we only get 6.9 percent of volume instead
of the full contribution. Also, you have to stay on top of the game
to control franchisees, you have to want to play, and you have to
get them to want to play because you can't use a stick to keep
them in line."

Getting franchisees to "want to play" is a major undertak-
ing, for it involves developing an emotional attachment to the
franchise system. During the course of my study, I found franchisees and franchisors alike had a rather dispassionate view of
franchising. I rarely heard positive attributions about franchising, nor did I hear unsolicited positive remarks toward others. I
never heard, for instance, franchisees say, "Wow, these guys are
great! They really know how to manage a franchise system. It's a
fantastic opportunity here." Similarly, I never heard franchisors
say, "We've got the best franchisees in franchising! We'll beat the
competition because of our people." Even when I asked point-
blank what they liked best about franchising, the answers were
far from passionate. For franchisors, the common response was
"the income." Among franchisees, the responses varied: "Being
your own boss," "The hours," "The other franchisees," and "It's
my own."

The last comment results from the entrepreneurial framework—or ideology—surrounding franchising. Franchisees are
likely to seek independence and autonomy from the franchisor
and to resist being monitored or told what to do. As one franchisee from Sign Masters stated, "I love to see new guys come

into the system because that's one more person to keep the franchisor off my back." Another franchisee from King Cleaners stated, "What do I want from my franchisor? I want them to leave me alone." Hence, the problem of control is the single greatest uncertainty facing the franchisor.

# CHAPTER 9

C O N T R O L

It is worth revisiting Bill Parker, the CEO of King Cleaners, for his insight on franchising. "Managers will do what you want," he said, "but they won't work hard; franchisees will work hard, but they won't do what you want." Although Parker's comment highlights the concern franchisors have with controlling the system, it is nonetheless a curious statement since franchisors have a contract that is exhaustive and slanted heavily in their favor.

In fact, it is so much in their favor that attorneys for franchisors have wondered why people even sign them. An attorney for a franchisor confided to me, "Lawyers that are unfamiliar with franchising just can't believe these contracts, they're astounded by what they find," he said. "I mean, you've seen them, they're like servitude—they're worse than servitude." In speaking with franchise attorneys, one can almost discern a sentiment of contempt toward franchisees for signing such a one-sided contract. One CEO stated, "Basically, franchising is a legal structure. Once a person signs the contract—and honestly, I don't know why anyone would—that's it. We've got him."

Yet in the three systems I studied, franchisors were the first to admit that they didn't have control over franchisees. "You have to handle problems different from the contract," stated Stu Beyer. "Once you bring up the contract, you're done." A franchise manager from Star Muffler stated, "We have a policy to negotiate a win-win situation with all franchisees. If that fails, we'll play hardball, but if it gets to that point we've lost. The contract is effective, but we only use it as a last resort. It has to be that we don't want a guy in our system at all before we bring up the contract."

It might seem that the key issue for franchisors would be to design a contract that was specific to each franchisee, for this may then solve the control problem. But this appears to be an unworkable solution. Even if one could develop a contract that took into account franchisee-specific assets, skills, and capabilities, as the number of franchisees and potential franchisees increased franchisors would incur significant costs. These costs would surely outweigh the benefits of franchisee-specific contracts. From a practical standpoint, a franchisee-specific contract may serve to rile franchisees because it implies franchisor favoritism. "We've had guys level that charge at us before," stated Mark Spinelli. "You can't give one guy a special deal because then you'd have to give everyone a special deal. We treat everybody the same. We have to."

"Why is that?" I asked.

"Let's face it. These guys talk to each other, and we promote that. That's one of the things that make a franchise system a system. We want these guys to share ideas, problems, and concerns with each other because we can't be out there all the time to help them whenever something comes up. Besides, if someone's found some solution to a problem, it's heard better by the other guys if it comes from a franchisee than if it comes from us."

"But can't they also talk about other things? Things that undermine you?"

"Yeah, and we understand that. We know that there are positive and negative attitudes and ideas out there. We promote the positive, but the negative exists, too."

"Is cheating a problem, do you think?"

"There isn't a shop in the system that doesn't underreport, and some of that's OK. But if it's a lot, then we'll go after a guy."

"Let's say there are two types of cheating, a guy can underreport income, or he can do something detrimental to the trademark. Which of these seems to be more of a problem at Star Muffler?" I asked.

"Well, both bother me. We don't have a big problem with either one. For the guy that underreports, we'll catch him. In the short term, he can get away with it, but we know what to look for and it'll turn up. It has in the past and will in the future."

"What are some of those things that you look for?"

"We've seen patterns that involve cheating. There are underlying problems, usually if a guy is involved with drugs, if he's got a drinking problem, or if he's going through a divorce. Those things are clear signals to us to look more carefully at his reports and what is going on in his shop. We monitor very closely, and we know the sales growth and whether those numbers are out of line. We try to help the guy get straightened around—we want him to be successful. We really run this business more like a nonprofit, and we think that it's our mission to help people get into business for themselves. If anything, we are too understanding, too weak. We're usually willing to give guys a second, third, and fourth chance. But if someone does something to devalue the trademark, we won't stand for that because that means a guy's not giving the full value to the customer."

At King Cleaners, the responses echoed those of Spinelli. But at Sign Masters, Stu Beyer had a different take on this: "Underreporting concerns me more. It's easier for them to do. Now, if they underreport by ten thousand dollars, that's OK." Another franchise manager at Sign Masters stated, "Underreporting is more of a problem. It wouldn't do them any good to hurt the name."

Perhaps Beyer's focus on the financial side of the business, to the exclusion of monitoring the trademark, was a contributing factor to the ultimate downfall of Sign Masters. Even so, they didn't do a terrific job monitoring the financials. As one franchisee said, "There's no way they can really monitor us. We don't carry that much inventory, and this is not a cash business. If there isn't a receipt, I don't report it." Another franchisee agreed, "Anybody can play with the books so that 14K in sales looks like

7K." Beyer also stated, "Control is not a big issue here. We operate on a team basis." But, whether or not Beyer recognizes it, control is the critical uncertainty in franchise systems.

## SURVEILLANCE

If the contract, which is decidedly one-sided, cannot control franchisees, then franchisors must resort to other means. One very obvious control mechanism is direct surveillance by being present in the unit during its operation. "You can learn a lot by being in the shop," stated Mark Spinelli, "but you have to be able to read between the lines, you have to understand the business. We've found that it isn't how many times you visit a shop, but the quality of those visits. People will tell you that you have to have secret shoppers and make surprise visits in order to find out if franchisees are following a system, but that's just not true and it's not fair. It is not the way we want to run our business. We tell a guy when we're going to visit him and I have to tell you, if a guy's cheating us, we'll find it no matter what. He won't be able to hide it."

Other managers at Star Muffler agreed with Spinelli on the importance of being at the shops, but they were more likely to use other methods as well. "We've sent in secret shoppers in the past," said a Star Muffler manager, "mainly into shops where we had reason to believe that our system was not being followed. We often use people to phone into a shop just to check that the proper procedure is being followed."

At Sign Masters, it was only store visits that allowed franchisors to monitor franchisees and, even then, to no real effect. "It's pretty difficult to control franchisees," stated Stu Beyer. "You can't see a store more than six times a year for a three-hour visit." There was nothing in Beyer's comments to indicate that he really understood the business and knew what to look for. If he had a better knowledge of the business, perhaps he wouldn't have needed six visits per store to monitor the system. In any case, franchisees at Sign Masters operated their business according to their own personal tastes. "There's not a good way that they can control us," stated a high-revenue franchisee. "We're free to market where we want, we can purchase where we want, and they can't control how we report our income."

The last comment, concerning the income statement, is a sure sign that Sign Masters does not have control of the system because income statements are the lifeblood of franchising. At Star Muffler and King Cleaners, income statements were required quarterly at a minimum and monthly for some franchisees. These statements were very effective tools for controlling the system. A manager at Star Muffler explained, "A monthly statement can tell you a whole lot. We look at them to determine if there are problems in pricing, if the mix of sales is what it should be. The sales tell us how thoroughly people inspect cars and also if people are asking the right questions of customers." A franchise manager at King Cleaners stated, "We look to see if the numbers make sense. Is the number accurate? Does the cost of goods, labor, or salary make sense?"

Beyond monthly income reports, franchisors have the right to conduct full audits for any franchisee, for any reason or no reason at all. John, the distributor at King Cleaners, was suspicious of Rusty primarily because Rusty was a "mover" and had taken a few liberties with business expenses. "I audited Rusty and found no problems, none at all. He runs his business different from everyone else, but the royalty comes off the gross sales and he doesn't underreport that. But he does quite well. Last year, he paid himself a six-figure salary and also put sixty thousand dollars in the bank." When I asked Rusty if he felt singled out because of the audit, he replied, "No. They can do that and I expect them to do that. I understand business a lot better than the other franchisees, and I think John was worried the IRS would catch me for something and that would slander the King Cleaners name and also deprive him of some royalties. But I'm not doing anything illegal."

Monitoring franchisees by being in the shop was an effective way to control the system, and it was used by franchisors both as a control mechanism and also as a reward. For instance, recall that Pete Morgan, the top revenue-producing franchisee at Star

Muffler, told me with a sheepish grin, "I don't know when the last time anybody from Corporate stopped by to see my shop. It's probably been something like three years ago. Look outside—I still have my original sign. That's thirteen years old, but they never say anything about it."

As a control mechanism, in-store visits can only be a partial control at best. It was not an effective control mechanism at King Cleaners since services were provided at the client's premises. Instead, King Cleaners called clients directly to seek feedback on franchisee performance. At Star Muffler and Sign Masters, in-store visits were more helpful to franchisors, but as the systems grew and franchise units became geographically dispersed, this method became too taxing and the visits could only be cursory. For example, if Stu Beyer really visited each of his thirty stores six times a year, as he claimed, he would have to send out an associate three or four days a week. Sign Masters clearly did not have the resources to do that, especially in the early start-up phase of the company.

A more effective tool for control is the required income statement. Not only did franchisees send in reports monthly (thereby minimizing corporate resources for travel), but the information gained by franchisors allowed them to better understand the business. Franchisors had at their disposal all of the reports of each franchisee, and they were able to make valid comparisons among franchisees. Beyond this, franchisors could use that information to better understand the growth and decline of specific franchise units, to learn about the markets in particular areas, and to gather information on the best practices from within their system. Not only did income statements help franchisors control the system regularly, but they provided them with knowledge about the business over the long term and allowed them to gain information about the cycles of the business, particular growth patterns of franchisees, and other nuances about the markets in which they operated. Such information advantages allow the sophisticated franchisor to control the system to a large extent.

## INCENTIVES

Another type of control mechanism is the monetary incentive. For instance, King Cleaners offers a discount on products to franchisees who pay on a timely basis. Rusty, from King Cleaners told me, "If you pay cash for your products, you get a 10 percent discount. If you pay by the tenth of the month, you get an additional 10 percent discount. Most of these guys don't do that, but they should, I mean, it's a 20 percent discount on products that you need to pay for anyway."

Another franchisee from King Cleaners explained how franchisor incentives controlled him. "First thing that they did, made sure I attended the [training] academy. Made sure I would go to the meetings. I can miss two monthly meetings and still get a 10 percent discount on products." Neither Star Muffler nor Sign Masters offered deep discounts on products similar to the policy at King Cleaners, however. At Sign Masters, franchisees were free to buy their supplies from any vendor, so the company lacked control over the product. At Star Muffler, everyone used the same approved vendor so the franchisor knew the inventory levels of each franchisee. But even so, it was only at King Cleaners that incentives played a role in controlling franchisees.

## THREATS

If the contract, direct supervision, and incentives did not effectively control franchisees, franchisors were left with few alternatives other than threats, implied or overt. Although threats take many forms, one common feature is that from the franchisee's perspective every threat appears credible. A franchisee from King Cleaners stated, "They make comments like 'You're using all King Cleaners chemicals, right?' The first thing they do when they come in for a visit is to look in the closet to make sure you're using King Cleaners stuff."

Another franchisee from King Cleaners explained to me how the franchisor made a credible threat: "I don't want you to take this the wrong way, but you're a college guy and you don't understand how it works. Think about it. Suppose you need products for a big job on the weekend. Friday the products don't come in. Lost in shipment or whatever. They can play any type of game they want to. They can delay paperwork. . . . If the MFC [the distributor] wants to go to bat for you, he'll go to bat for you. If he wants you to hang out to dry, you go out to dry.

"They have a free hand in running their business in any way they want. The Q/A (Quality Assurance) Program can be as tough as the MFC wants to make it—it's a tool they can vary to their ends. A couple of years ago they brought a franchisee to court, and they dragged it out for three years. They didn't win, but they scared the hell out of three thousand guys."

"Did this ever happen to you? Have you ever had your shipments held up?" I asked.

"Well, no. But it could happen. They can jack you as bad as they want."

Another implied threat is that future transactions will not run in the franchisee's favor. A franchisee from Star Muffler stated, "I didn't get into this business to only have one shop. I want to own at least two or maybe more, and I want them to all be close to each other. I could have bought two units at a (much larger) competitor, but they wanted to sell me one in Kentucky and one in Montana. Anyway, Corporate won't sell me another unit until this one reaches certain targets, and they want me to put in a new sign and another bay. That'll cost me a helluva lot of money. They can stand in my path of growth, how quickly I can expand."

Sometimes the threat is more than implied, as a franchisee from King Cleaners learned. "They threaten you. They have the power to not give your license back. They'll say, 'You know, we can take your franchise away.'" Another franchisee stated, "They ask you questions like, 'If you're not going to grow your business, what are you going to do? What's your long-term picture? If you're not going to grow your business, then maybe you should sell it.'"

At Star Muffler, the threat was credible since the company had in the past brought franchisees to court for violations of the contract. Moreover, Star Muffler also punished franchisees that underreported.

Mark Spinelli once confided to me, "You know, Darrell used to have two franchise units."

"No, I didn't know that," I replied.

"Yeah, we caught him stealing from us, so we took one of his units away as punishment."

This was such a successful response that the newest franchisee in the system admitted to me, "Spinelli's a businessman. He's a nice guy, but if you screw him over, he'll turn on you like a snake." Predictably, another franchisee from Star Muffler responded, "How do they control me? They demand it. Period. The end. They infer that there's a possibility that they'll pull the franchise, especially without any money back."

In addition to threats, franchisors use their interactions with franchisees to reinforce their status in the system. One franchisee from King Cleaners said, "Their control is more subtle. They have an image of who is a good franchisee. There's an in and out feeling here. You're not inside unless you're toeing their personal and business values." A franchisee from Star Muffler summed up best how the subtle forms of control continue to work long after the interaction had ceased: "I wish they wouldn't look down at us all the time, the old blue-collar, white-collar thing. They've always made me feel like I don't know what I'm doing. One time they said to me, 'We view all you franchisees as a bunch of potential lawsuits.' Can you believe that? I don't know . . . Sometimes I feel like I really don't own the shop."

Franchisors preferred to use reason, including incentives, to control franchisees. As Mark Spinelli said, "We can use a stick to control these guys, but we'd rather use honey." If the honey fails, there were always threats. But in many respects, if franchisors managed the system well at the start and continued to manage it well, then neither legal action nor threats should be necessary measures.

INTERACTIONS

In addition to, or in lieu of, contracts, surveillance, incentives, and threats, franchisors control their franchisee units through the many subtle interactions that they have with franchisees. These interactions start during the initial meeting between franchisees and corporate staff, extend through training, and continue during the on-going relationship between franchisors and franchisees. The quality, frequency, and intensity of visits, the thoroughness and frequency of audits, even the speed of response by the franchisor to franchisee requests—have cumulative effects on the overall relationship and serve to keep franchisees under control. Perhaps the most effective method of control is to develop a belief system that is shared by both franchisors and franchisees. Stu Beyer of Sign Masters stated, "They have to believe in the system the same way we do. If they don't believe in the system then it's impossible to manage, and they should probably think about leaving."

"How do you get them to believe in the system? Do you look for something while you recruit them?" I asked.

"No," he responded, "it's difficult to recruit selectively because you can't tell who is going to do well. If you start off right, it sure makes it easier later." Added one franchisee from Star Muffler, "They don't have to control me. My beliefs and their beliefs are the same." Mark Spinelli of Star Muffler also emphasized the importance of start-up training for this. "Training is a process, not an event. We've found that we have to continually reinforce our system to these guys. If we were to just give them the training once during the initial three-week training session, we'd never have compliance with the system."

"Well," I asked, "how do you control franchisees?"

"Not control," he responded, "but achievement of goals. We're in the people business, and as a sideline to that we also fix cars."

"What do you think about the following quote," I asked, " 'Managers will do what you want, but they won't work hard. Franchisees will work hard, but they won't do what you want?' "

Spinelli laughed, then grew serious and said, "I don't agree with that. Maybe what you tell the franchisee doesn't work. You've got to give guys the ability to adapt to the local market, and that means giving up some control—letting them make the decisions they need to make to be competitive in their market. The culture that existed here before we bought the firm was one where you don't want to tell a guy what he's doing wrong so you can blame him."

The training program at Star Muffler immersed the franchisee into the processes and procedures of the business and, as Spinelli remarked, it did not end when the training session terminated. This continual process was understood by all franchisees. A long-time franchisee said, "They try to control us, but with our longevity they leave us alone. We're not on a leash like the new guys." The effectiveness of Spinelli's continual training was that franchisees learned that there would only be one way to operate the business. As one franchisee commented, "Everybody fights them in the beginning. Either you come around or get out."

At King Cleaners, John, the master distributor, remarked, "We don't try to control people. We have monthly meetings, and it is strongly recommended that franchisees attend. Mostly, those meetings are informative and provide a learning experience for franchisees—both from me and from some of the things that others are doing in the market that seem to be working. If people stop going to those meetings, then I know that we've got a problem. That's the first sign that they aren't making it."

While Star Muffler made a concerted effort in training, monitoring, and face-to-face interactions to continually promote its system, King Cleaners's laissez-faire approach accomplished the same thing. One long-time franchisee told me, "There's not a lot of heavy-handed control here. The philosophy at King Cleaners is to let the marketplace take care of poor quality. Once the revenue goes down and a guy goes under, they put a new one in place."

But at Sign Masters neither the market nor the franchisor

controlled franchisees. When I asked franchisees how the company controlled them, they responded, "He can't" or "They don't." One franchisee with high sales said, "This particular business is not like very many others. It is not labor-intensive, and there is not a lot of inventory. Even the inventory we have is fairly generic, I mean, vinyl is vinyl. Because it's business-to-business, the payments are invoices, purchase orders and the like. Very little cash goes through the store. If people don't ask for a receipt, I don't report it, but that's never more than one hundred dollars a month. They're not out here like watchdogs. As long as the store is clean they seem to be satisfied."

The lack of control over the franchise system was the leading cause of Sign Masters' precarious financial position. However, the company's inability to control the system was only partially due to the nature of the sign industry. More important, the lack of control, which was not shared by King Cleaners nor Star Muffler, hinged on Beyer's inability to foster one particularly critical relationship: trust.

TRUST

Of all the relationships franchisors can develop with franchisees, none is more critical to maintaining control than trust. It is the social lubricant that allows parties to take risks that they might not otherwise take—and at a speed that they might not otherwise pursue. It is particularly important within franchise systems to have a strong level of trust since franchisees are geographically dispersed and face-to-face contact is not always possible. Because of an ideology of entrepreneurship, franchisees are often independent-minded and likely to follow their own instincts in the business. Franchisors face the challenge of "having to say the same message thirty different ways," as a manager at Star Muffler stated, and high levels of trust allow the message to be implemented faster, even if it is not fully understood nor agreed with completely.

The relationship between trust and control was not lost on either party: One franchisor commented on ways to control franchisees: "I try to get their trust in me." But for many franchisees the issue of whom to trust was not a choice, but a matter of necessity, as a franchisee from Star Muffler stated earlier: "I got to trust them. They got me right where I don't want to be."

But franchisors do not have to reciprocate that trust, and the lack of reciprocity lays the seeds for latent conflict. Said a franchisee from Star Muffler, "I've proven myself time and time again because my receipts match me. If they don't trust a person like me, then I don't belong with them and they don't belong in business."

It might seem that franchisees would be more likely to trust other franchisees rather than the franchisor. After all, regardless of their location, sales, or experience, franchisees are in a structurally similar position vis-à-vis the franchisor. But trust is a difficult relationship to cultivate, and the nature of franchising makes it an unlikely result, at least on a large scale.

Part of the reason lies in the sheer amount of available time franchisees have to develop relationships. As one franchisee noted, "It's difficult to find any time to talk to the other franchisees when you spend sixty hours a week working." In addition, franchisees end up competing with each other, and it is difficult, perhaps unwise, to trust a competitor.

To be sure, some franchisees were considered trustworthy, and this was evident in the work I carried out. But for the most part, franchisors were the most trusted members of the organization. I asked one franchisee why he trusted the franchisor. He said, "You've got to trust somebody going into this." At King Cleaners and Star Muffler that sentiment was widespread, because Mark Spinelli at Star Muffler and John and Barbara at King Cleaners were the most trusted members of the system. But at Sign Masters that was not the case. Neither Stu Beyer nor any of his managers were highly trusted. "They've started and stopped so many marketing programs," one franchisee stated, "that it makes it really hard to trust anything they say." Another franchisee said, "I don't know. They've had so many personnel changes just in the last eighteen months, I don't trust any of those people."

For others, the franchisor appeared to be stealing ideas. "I get nervous when they come in here—not because I'm doing anything wrong, but because I feel like I'm being watched. They ask questions that lead me to believe they don't know much about the business. I don't trust them to teach me anything about the business, and their track record in marketing is horrible."

Beyer's trust level plummeted even further after an annual meeting. "You know we had our annual meeting not too long ago," stated one franchisee, "and we spent the entire day listening to a supplier tell us about the properties of vinyl. Beyer didn't address us once—the whole meeting was the supplier. I don't want to know about the properties of vinyl if the company is going bankrupt! He needs to include us in the financial conditions of the company. We've heard so many rumors for so long, we've seen the changes in personnel, we know he put his house on the market and moved into an apartment. But he said nothing. I don't trust him for anything."

Who was trusted at Sign Masters? Primarily, the high-revenue franchisees. In fact, the top three or four franchisees at Sign Masters achieved the same status and occupied the same position as Mark Spinelli at Star Muffler and John at King Cleaners.

FRANCHISEE CONTROL

Franchisors have several options to control franchisees, but what about the reverse? Are there ways that franchisees can control the franchisor? I asked franchisees and franchisors about this possibility, and here the agreement was unanimous: Franchisees will not be able to control the franchisor. Mark Spinelli of Star Muffler stated, "No, they can't—not in the long-term. We've been manipulated before, but we're big enough now that we won't stand for it."

"How big an impact does the largest franchisee have?"

"Not even 7 percent of our revenues are dependent on the largest franchisee and as we get bigger, as we add more shops, this number declines."

Stu Beyer of Sign Masters said, "They push us to see how far we'll go." But there is a big difference between how franchisees and franchisors control each other, because franchisees *attempt* to control the franchisor, while the franchisor actually does have control.

Most franchisees were emphatic in their responses about their inability to control the franchisor:

"No. You can't."

"There's no way."

"The have an ironclad agreement in their favor."

"I don't know that you can."

"No. You'll never do it."

"It's tough to do—impossible. They got you over a barrel."

"There's really no way until you become a big franchisee . . . [A]ll you can do is suggest."

"I'm not a strong enough voice to be heard."

"I can't. I have to trust them. They got me right where I don't want to be. They can make or break me."

But some franchisees did have a plan to control the franchisor:

"I allowed myself to be elected to the advisory council because I want to start a dealer association."

"You could rally support from the other franchisees."

"I try to use constructive criticism."

"By being a team player and standing up for what's right."

"Delay royalties."

"Not part-taking of the marketing programs. Hold up royalties."

"Withhold royalties—it's almost like going on strike."

Despite the optimism of a few franchisees, the fact remains that franchisors are resolved to remain independent from the control of franchisees, and there are few avenues available to franchisees to pierce this resolve. Withholding royalties could be particularly risky since doing so provides the franchisor with ample grounds for termination. Even binding together into an association is likely to raise concerns from franchisors.

I posed this question to franchisors: "Would it bother you if the franchisees formed a council or group to band together in negotiations with you?"

Predictably, all franchisors were strongly opposed to any such efforts by franchisees. Stu Beyer of Sign Masters became agitated and stated, "That goes counter to the concept of the whole franchise system. That's what the advertising council is for." Mark Spinelli of Star Muffler commented, "Yes, it would really bother me. If they were to come to us as a group, we would not acknowledge them." Another manager at Star Muffler said, "That would bother me. It would mean that we're not doing our job."

Such associations are unlikely to arise, however. Each company already had an advisory council, and if franchisees attempted to band together the franchisor could respond, "You already have an advisory council to voice your concerns. If you don't like the job they're doing, take it up with them."

A more likely reason franchisees did not band together was that it goes counter to their own personal beliefs that they are entrepreneurs, that they are independent. Most franchisees viewed themselves as entrepreneurs, and by believing this they foiled any attempts to bind together since entrepreneurship is an independent and solitary endeavor. The relative isolation of franchisees, coupled with their independent perspective, blinds them to the reality that they have much in common due to the structural underpinnings of the strategy. These structural components, which go largely unnoticed, also work in ways that control the system.

## STRUCTURAL SOURCES OF CONTROL

The control mechanisms that franchisors exerted were mainly functions of the relationship they established with franchisees. That is, incentives, threats, training systems, and trust were all under the influence of franchisors, and they were elements that

franchisors directly managed. There are other control mechanisms that, because they are inherent to franchising, cannot be
directly influenced by franchisors but nonetheless serve to control franchisees. These mechanisms, while not completely understood by franchise participants, nevertheless impacted them
significantly.

For instance, trademarks controlled a franchise system in
several ways. Trademarks strip franchisees of their individuality
and set the system's boundaries, not only the physical boundaries, but also the scope of acceptable practices that franchisees
could undertake. In essence, trademarks forced franchisees to
adopt standard procedures but these procedures could be at
odds with what worked best in a franchisee's local market. When
a franchisee enters into a system, he or she gives up control
over aspects of the business and instead agrees to operate the
business to the franchisor's standards. If the market and the
trademark are perfectly matched, franchisees should have few
problems, but if their location differed in some significant way,
the trademark would prevent franchisees from adapting to and
meeting the challenges of the market.

Trademarks, because of their brand image and implied consistency, function identically for all members of the franchise
system and thereby create a system of perfect substitutes. Consequently, it is only the price for services offered and the location at which they are delivered that set franchisees apart. In reality, trademarks create interdependencies among franchisees
and give rise to the potential for free-riders.[1] That is, because
the trademark applies to everybody in the system, franchisees
who do nothing to build the trademark receive the same benefits as those who do a lot to promote the trademark. In short,
trademarks not only help the franchisor control the delivery and
scope of services franchisees provide, but they also function in a
way that levels franchisees, bringing down the best franchisees
to the level of the lowest common denominator. Perhaps this is

1. For an introduction to the free-rider problem, see Mancur Olson, *The Logic of
Collective Action: Public Goods and the Theory of Groups* (Cambridge: Harvard University Press, 1965).

why Rusty of King Cleaners, when asked about the value of the trademark, surprisingly said, "It hurts."

Another structural feature of franchise systems that aided control was the route or career path franchisees embarked upon prior to entering a franchise system. Like most structural sources of control, the importance of career paths as a control mechanism remained hidden from both franchisors and franchisees. Yet, how franchisees entered into franchise systems, where in the occupational structure they entered from, and how they financed their purchase all converged to provide information advantages to the franchisor. For the franchisees that entered franchise systems blindly, with no (or little) prior information about the franchise, franchisors gained control through the asymmetry in information. But even if franchisees knew the franchisor beforehand, they often had little direct experience in owning a business and knew little about the industry. In fact, over 90 percent of the franchisees knew nothing about franchising as a method of business before entering.

Finally, since many franchisees depleted a large proportion of their savings in buying a franchise, they had great incentives to succeed. Failure resulted in extensive personal loss, both in terms of financial capital but also in terms of time invested in the failed unit. Franchisors not only know the financial capabilities of entering franchisees, but they know when a unit is breaking even or making money. Hence, franchisors may take the full financial disclosure that franchisees submit and use that information to their own advantage.

The final structural source of control that was inherent to, or endemic to, franchising stemmed from the nature of work franchisees carried out. Indeed, the very environment in which franchisees operated provided a powerful means of control to franchisors. Franchisees worked in turbulent environments and faced severe uncertainties in labor inputs and service output.

On one hand, the precarious environment could provide incentives for franchisees to shirk and operate outside of the trademark, but on the other hand, the environment almost assured franchisors that franchisees would have to expend great time and effort to remain solvent. In doing so, franchisees were hindered in their ability to form social relationships with other franchisees. And since they subscribed to an ideology of entrepreneurship, they directed their energies not toward a collectivist orientation but instead toward independence, autonomy, and individual gain.

The fact remains that the ideology of entrepreneurship is pervasive. Franchisees enter a system governed by a long-term, ironclad contract in the franchisor's favor, operate on the periphery of the economy providing services that are largely generic and subject to price competition, and shroud themselves under a trademark that makes their unit a perfect substitute.

It is a system that challenges franchisees on all fronts.

# CHAPTER 10

EPILOGUE

Shortly after the end of the window-washer demonstration with which I opened this book and Tom from Central had left the premises, the franchisees at King Cleaners turned on the unit and began to wash the very same windows they had refused to wash earlier. One franchisee pointed the hose toward the ground and said, "I wonder if this thing is powerful enough to clean the parking lot?" The other franchisees laughed at this idea, but when the franchisee quickly cleaned grease and oil stains, they became quite interested.

"Hey," one shouted, "let's take it over to that cement landing around the back of the building and see if it can clean that."

So about ten guys picked up the washer and wheeled it toward the back of the parking lot. They began to spray the cement landing, which was filthy from the cars and trucks that parked there while people unloaded their luggage. Again, they were quite surprised to see the landing could easily be cleaned by using the power sprayer.

"Is there a very big market for this?" I asked a franchisee near me as we watched various people taking turns with the washer.

"Yeah, you bet," he stated. "Cleaning driveways, garages, parking lots—well, any paved surface, really, is kinda hard. It takes a lot of muscle, a lot of scrubbing to get anything clean. This would help a lot in that market."

"I'm surprised Central didn't think of that," I stated.

"I'm not," he quipped. "They just sprung this on us today. They never consulted us or asked us to look at the washer. If they had, maybe the sales pitch by Tom would have gone differently. The way they went about it, no one was really interested in the thing. But if we'd known that it could double as a pavement washer, it could have generated a lot more interest."

"Are you going to buy one?"

"Me? I don't think so. I'm not really interested in that market, but I'll wait and see what kind of pricing they come up with and what incentives they give to us," he replied, as the franchisees slowly filed back into the convention center.

The entire window washer episode reveals, in abbreviated form, many of the fundamental features of franchise systems. It reveals a profile of the people who deliver franchised products and services and underscores how difficult it is for franchisors to motivate them. More important, the demonstration highlights the critical uncertainty of control and the organizational problem of change. These fundamental features are in sharp contrast to accepted notions of franchising.

Indeed, franchise systems are typically portrayed in one of two ways. On one hand, it is commonplace to read derisive commentaries that bemoan the franchising of America and the loss of the individual retailer, the family-owned business. Franchise systems, because of standardization and mass production of services, are purported to stifle the creativity and uniqueness of regional businesses so that small towns as well as urban areas are much the same. On the other hand, there is an equally prevalent view that franchising guarantees wealth to all participants and that franchisees are therefore enormously successful and their businesses profitable.

Both views are benighted. The first perspective is in error because it views franchising as synonymous with large global corporations and ignores the more common circumstance of most franchise companies. Franchise companies are rather small in scope, have a regional rather than a national or global presence, and are largely populated with franchisees earning average returns and modest incomes. Moreover, many—if not most—franchisees operated their business with a spouse, child, or sibling so the family-owned business did not disappear, but instead transformed from one rather obvious form to a more subtle one. Likewise, the second view of franchising disregards the experience of the vast majority of franchisees. While there are some franchisees who are successful, there are many others who fail or barely eke out an existence.

In the eyes of those in the franchising system, franchising figures very differently from what one expects based on preconceived and ill-informed notions of it. Although franchise systems have as their hallmark the consistent delivery of relatively standardized products and services, there is nothing standardized about managing them, and the systems themselves are unique, idiosyncratic, subject to uncertainties, and difficult to control. It is ironic that a business strategy that has the consistent and reliable delivery of products and services as its core would, because of these factors, suffer from the severe uncertainty of control. This critical uncertainty stems not from the trademark, products, or services, but from the franchisees on the delivery end of the equation. It is the role of the franchisee as mediator between the product or service and the customer that raises havoc with franchisors. This uncertainty does not occur because franchisees are belligerent, recalcitrant, or uncooperative, but rather because no single management strategy works for all franchisees.

People enter franchise systems with particular backgrounds and experiences and from particular locations in the occupational structure. They enter with prior views of franchising, with beliefs about the value of trademarks, the amount of assistance they will need or want, and a wide range of other ideas over which franchisors have little control. The diversity of franchisees is the major source of uncertainty because they cannot be reduced to a single profile.

At least three different types of franchisee—neo-franchisees, disillusioned, and sideliners—can be found in franchise systems. These groups differ in their educational backgrounds, amount of financial capital at their disposal, and professional goals. Most important, franchisees enter a system with their own aspirations, highly individual expectations for themselves and their business, and values that may not be easily reconciled with the system of the franchisor.

The diversity among franchisees in background, aspirations, expectations, and values does not cause the problem of control but can contribute to it through the equally pressing problem of organizational alignment. With any highly diverse population, there exists the potential for differences in interests—for a wedge to emerge—and the difference between franchisors and franchisees is no less real. The wedge in interests is exacerbated by the ideology of entrepreneurship, one of the fundamental underpinnings of the strategy.

Franchisees largely believe themselves to be entrepreneurs because they "take all the risk," and this belief is perpetuated by franchisors that promote the sale of units as "owning your own business." But because franchisees and franchisors believe that franchising is an entrepreneurial pursuit, numerous problems ensue. Franchisors constantly must manage a person who will not take advice or will do so only slowly and begrudgingly. Obviously, change within the system is an arduous task.

The fundamental features of franchising, multiple profiles, differences in values, misalignment of interests, and an entrepreneurial ideology combine to render control of the system a critical uncertainty facing franchisors. However, these elements are further compounded by the simple yet salient fact that franchisees are geographically dispersed. Taken together, the fundamental features and dispersion provide the motive and opportunity, respectively, for franchisees to operate their unit outside of the trademark.

CONTRACT OR CONTACT?

The organizational problems of control and commitment are not novel, nor are they endemic to franchising alone. I opened this monograph by noting that in the Middle Ages a sovereign would trust a high Church official to collect taxes and other monies in a franchiselike arrangement. The Church official had status, an official position and, presumably, the value of honesty. Together these elements converged to lessen problems of control. But in this day and age, they do not converge within franchise systems, and consequently, control is particularly severe, onerous, and of paramount importance.

In fact, control is the crux of the problem facing franchisors, and it must be solved or they will face the same fate as Stu Beyer of Sign Masters. Ironclad contracts were not enough to save his business. Although Beyer made several blunders, his inability to control the system stemmed from a laissez faire approach to franchising, one in which he afforded franchisees too much freedom in operating their units. This was not due to laziness on his part; rather, it derived from his belief in the inherent trustworthiness of individuals. "We're not big into control," he once said to me. "We operate on a team basis."

This belief that franchisees would operate honestly, coupled with his deeply held belief that the trademark was invaluable, blinded him to the possibility that franchisees would operate in ways detrimental to the trademark. "It wouldn't do them any good to hurt the name," he stated. Beyer never really had control of his system; indeed, the system had control of him.

On the other hand, Star Muffler exercised nearly complete control over the system. Spinelli and his executives knew franchisees and potential franchisees well; they understood every aspect of their system, industry, and franchising. Armed with this knowledge, Star Muffler enjoyed a significant degree of control over the system. They also controlled one critical asset in their business, the land. Spinelli once remarked to me, "I can't stress how important it is to control the real estate. I can't see how a franchisor can make it if he doesn't control the real estate. We can get these guys out. We still have to go through the legal system, but it's a lot quicker and less expensive since we own the real estate."

Finally, Spinelli controlled the system by stressing over and over again that franchising is rent of a license to operate under the Star Muffler trademark according to its standards—nothing more, nothing less. Spinelli's autocratic approach seemed to work well with franchisees for it was a management style that was taken for granted and largely accepted by them. As one franchisee stated, "A lot of these people in franchising, that's what they want, is power."

There is a third alternative to the laissez faire and autocratic extremes, the social capital approach to control. Rather than provide franchisees with an unfettered license to operate as they please or control them completely because of property rights, franchisors can foster productive relationships. This is the approach that John from King Cleaners employed. In essence, he chose to increase the social capital of the system in order to achieve control of it. John had developed a high level of trust with nearly every franchisee in the system, and trust was not demanded, but earned. Although trust is a difficult relationship to develop and involves personal risk taking, the benefits to be gained are immeasurable. As one franchisee stated, "They don't have to control me. My beliefs and their beliefs are the same."

If franchisors and franchisees share normative values and a belief system, and have high levels of trust, then control over franchisees through the contract or other measures would be largely irrelevant; and contracts themselves, unnecessary. In the absence of these integrative mechanisms, franchisors are left with few devices to control the system other than the ones I have discussed.

So how do franchisors control the system? With every means possible. They train franchisees, provide incentives, monitor activities, require financial reports, threaten, and litigate. In short, franchisors use every tool in their power to bring franchisees in line. But despite an exhaustive agreement in their favor, it is not enough precisely because profiles of franchisees are not absolutes, interests of franchisors and franchisees are not as tightly aligned as they could be, and direct supervision of franchisees is not obtainable. The critical problem of controlling geographically dispersed workers is tractable for those franchisors who establish high levels of trust with franchisees. For those who cannot achieve that, the problem of control is a never-ending battle.

# INDEX